USA Based
Wholesale Directory

Compiled by   Diana Loera

TABLE OF CONTENTS

TABLE OF CONTENTS CONTINUED

Introduction

If you've been thinking about starting your own small business such as at your local flea market, you may have experienced the same problems that I did when trying to find wholesale sources. I started gathering information on wholesale sources after looking for such a directory and not finding one.

My husband and I had opened a booth at a local flea market. We had considerable sales success immediately and found our business was expanding rapidly.

With our expansion, we wanted to add more merchandise. I spent hours each week looking for companies that sold items that could be re-sold at flea markets.

As I started compiling various resources, it crossed my mind that I could save others the countless hours of time that I had spent by compiling all the sources in a directory. After several months I had gathered over 500 different sources of US based wholesale contacts.

As I grew up a "farmer's daughter" in the Midwest, I know a lot of people who for one reason or another prefer buying from companies that are based in the US. I also know people who are okay with ordering merchandise from outside the US.

Instead of having a mega directory of all wholesale sources, I created two directories – the one that you are reading today – USA Based Wholesale Directory and the soon to be released Wholesale Directory for Flea Market Vendors.

The USA Based Wholesale Directory contains over 500 listings with company name, a brief description and a web site address. The listings are divided into groups such as automotive, health and beauty, as seen on TV etc. Some listings may be in more than one category. Please keep in mind businesses open and close daily. There may be companies listed that are no longer in business. If so, please let us know so we can make changes to the directory.

This directory was laid out so that there is room to make brief notes on each page. I have also included a page at the back of the directory for your notes so that you are able to keep all information in the directory for easy reference.

About the Author

Diana Loera is an entrepreneur with over twenty years in the direct response marketing industry. She has worked with numerous companies as a rainmaker, media consultant and call center consultant. She also owns a media agency.

As part of a research pilot program to generate streams of income in what has been a very shaky economy, Diana created two additional companies, one of which was a flea market business.

The basis of the pilot program was to set up profitable companies on a shoestring budget.

Within a month of opening, she was able to hire someone to sell the merchandise for her and within two months of opening, she doubled her booth space. At this time she is looking for additional flea markets in the area to duplicate her success.

Diana lives in the Midwest with her husband, their dog and four cats.

As Seen On TV Products

As seen on TV infomercial products are hot sellers. Infomercials companies can make millions of dollars selling these products on late might TV. There are many people who may see the infomercial and even write down the number but not take action. Selling products such as these will attract that type of buyer.

Salco Distributors LLC
Your AS SEEN ON TV Products all under one roof. Make money buying products below retail.
www.ezdropshipper.com

AsSeenonTV.com
AsSeenOnTV.com is the largest "As Seen On TV" superstore offers a wide range of over 800 of the finest products.
www.asseenontv.com

Telebrands Wholesale
Buy from TelebrandsWholesale.com for all As Seen On TV wholesale products. No case minimums. Wholesale merchandise may be purchase with a credit card. Fast shipping.
www.telebrandswholesale.com

As Seen On TV Products Continued

Cossette Promotions
Our company has been in the retail and wholesale business since 1986. Our goal has always been to offer quality, reliable and fast service. Our offices and warehouse are located in one facility, allowing most orders to be shipped the same day.
www.cossettepromotions.com

OnTel Products
Ontel Products Corporation, your best source for "As Seen on TV" products. We are a leading manufacturer and distributor of the newest and best-selling "TV" products on the market.
www.ontelwest.com

Crossland Inc.
We are mainly a wholesaler and distributor of closeouts and As Seen on TV items.
www.crosslandinc.com

As Seen On TV Products Continued

Euroshine USA

Euroshine USA Inc. The Ultimate Cleaning Line. Ice Dream, Lycra Slimming Pants, Lycra Slimming Sports Bra, Sports Bra, bra push up bra, slimming pants, Microfiber products, Siroflex water products, Nowa cookware, PVA products, cleaners, brooms, diet weight loss and many more.
www.euroshine.net

As Seen On TV Wholesale

Get current top selling As Seen on TV products directly from the product manufacturer in wholesale quantities at wholesale prices

www.asseenontvwholesale.com

Automotive

More and more people are keeping their cars longer. Our down economy has caused an increase in people buying extended warranties and trying to fix as much as possible themselves. Auto parts are always popular traffic stoppers at flea markets and with a down economy they are even more popular.

Wholesale Truck Parts
Quality products, same day shipping and competitive pricing. Need an odd part we will find it for you. Catalog available. Specialize in hard to find parts.
www.wholesaletruckparts.com

TruckPerformance.com, Inc.
We maintain the world's largest online selection of truck aftermarket performance parts and accessories. We will not offer low quality, low price alternatives that sacrifice value and compromise customer satisfaction.
www.truckperformance.com

Air Dynamic Racing
Air Dynamic Racing offers top-notch service to the wholesale sector of the performance market, providing a well-known product line that is affordable, innovative, and of high quality.
www.airdynamicracing.com

Automotive Continued

R.R. Lalena Corp
From unique scented air fresheners, car detailing products, chemicals, car mats, dashboard accessories to DVD home theater systems, we are your one and only source for all wholesale car wash supplies and auto care needs.
www.rrlalena.com

MIMOUSA
MIMOUSA is a manufacturer and distributor of high quality aftermarket car parts and accessories.
www.mimousa.com

Video Games

Video gaming has grown in leaps and bounds the past few years. New games come out daily and carry hefty price tags. People who play video games are often looking for the best prices and will become repeat buyers.

Eagle Entertainment
Eagle Entertainment Inc. is a wholesale video game distributor. For over a decade we have been doing our best to find the most complete selection of video games, even the most difficult special requests, & offering them at wholesale prices to video stores & commercial outlets across the country.
www.regalgames.com

Northern Lights Distribution
Northern Lights is a distributor of consumer oriented electronic and entertainment products specializing in placement to small and alternative retail locations.
www.northernlightsdistribution.com

Pacific Games
Pacific Games is a distributor of video games and game accessories.
www.pacificgames.com

Real Games
PSX and Nintendo 64 wholesale video games, systems and accessories for commercial outlets.
www.real-games.com

Tommo Inc.
Tommo maintains an extensive catalog of video games and related merchandises for all of today's top gaming systems.
www.tommo.com

DVDs & Music

As with video games, the music and movie industry has exploded over the past few years.   Competition is steep among stores selling music and people are always shopping for the best prices.   People will often stop to dig through a stack of DVDs or CDs hoping to find movies or music that they have wanted to buy at an affordable price.   Repeat customers may be common if the prices and selection are good.

Super D
Super D specializes in fulfillment of audio and video products, as well as Super File audio and video database products.
www.sdcd.com

J's Records & Tapes
For over 21 years we have been providing a reliable source of quality music and videos. Our complete line includes CD's, videos and CD-ROMS.
www.jsrecord.com

Ingram Entertainment
Ingram Entertainment Inc. services over 10,000 retail accounts including video specialty stores, Internet retailers, drugstores and supermarkets.
www.ingramentertainment.com

Baker & Taylor
Baker & Taylor has been providing quality information and entertainment services. Baker & Taylor is a leading supplier of books, video, and music products for libraries and retailers worldwide.
www.btol.com

DVDs & Music Continued

Allegiant Marketing

At WholesaleMusicCDs.com we wholesale a combination of new release, popular artist, and quality discount music CDs. The CDs we distribute are all new and sealed. We are not like your traditional wholesale one stop we are a wholesale music service.
www.wholesalemusiccds.com

Horizons Records

Horizons Records sells in print, out of print, and hard to find CDs, cassettes, and LPs. Please come take a look at our varied selection.
www.cdlps.com

Glory Days Entertainment

Glory Days Entertainment is a family owned retail and wholesale distributor of classic and rare movies on DVD.
www.glorydaysentertainment.com

Frontier Video

Frontier Video is a new and used DVD and new and used VHS distributor for both retail and wholesale customers.
www.frontiervideo.com

DVDs & Music Continued

Arrow Distributing
Arrow Distributing Company is a rack jobber that provides merchandising, distribution and inventory management services to college bookstores, mass merchants, hypermarkets and public libraries.
www.arrdis.com

WaxWorks Inc.
Wax Works is one of the leading entertainment wholesale distributors in the nation. We service video retail, specialty stores and libraries.
www.waxworksonline.com

Distribution Video
Distribution Video & Audio is your complete one stop source for VHS videos, DVDs, music CDs, etc.
www.dvacloseouts.com

Norwalk Distributors
music & video DVD/CD/accessory wholesale distributor.
www.norwalkdist.com

DVDs & Music Continued

Vidtape
One stop shop for all your DVD, music CDs and video needs.
www.vidtape.com

Newtown Video Dist.
Newtown Video Distributors has been one of the leading and most respected used and new film distributors in the industry for over 15 years. We buy and sell new and used movies.
www.newtownvideo.com

Video Movie Wholesalers
New & used movies VHS & DVD. 20,000 new and used movie titles to choose from. 100% quality guaranteed.
www.usedmovies.com

DVD MegaPacks.com
DVDMegaPacks.com, where you can build your classic movie collection for 60 cents per movie. Relive the Golden Age of Cinema with our 50 Movie MegaPacks.
www.dvdmegapacks.com

DVDs & Music Continued

Video Group Distributors
We specialize in supplying complete video store opening packages from our 100,000 videos, games and DVD inventory.
www.videogroup.com

CE Distributors
CE Distributors Inc. specializes in Latino audio and video products. Wholesale orders only are accepted.
www.tejanomusic.com

VPD Inc.
Video Products Distributors is one of the leading providers of prerecorded videocassettes and digital video discs to the video retail industry.
www.vpdinc.com

Statco One Stop
US based black gospel music distributor. Shipping to customers worldwide. All labels, top hits, cds and videos.
www.statcoonestop.com

DVDs & Music Continued

Dart Distributing
As a full-service distributor of video, audio, computer software, console games, specialty books and entertainment titles, we help retailers offer the home entertainment titles consumers are looking for.
www.dartdist.com

White Swan Music
White Swan is a music label and an independent wholesale music distributor located in the foothills of the Rocky Mountains.
www.whiteswanmusic.com

Bayside Entertainment Distribution
Bayside Entertainment Distribution is a full-service, national distributor of independent music labels.
www.baysidedist.com

JM Distribution
Increase the inventory for your video business. Buy DVDs at wholesale prices direct.
www.jmdistribution.net

Latino

Hispanics are now the largest ethnic minority in the United States and during the past decade, U.S. Hispanic purchasing power has rapidly increased.

CE Distributors
CE Distributors Inc. specializes in Latino audio and video products. Wholesale orders only are accepted.
www.tejanomusic.com

El Paso Saddleblanket
Dealers and stores needed to sell our fine hand-woven southwest design wool rugs, saddle blankets, wall hangings & saddle blankets.
www.elpasosaddleblanket.com

Importaciones Mexico
Wholesale of German silver buckles, belts, wallets and western wear accessories. Our products are imported from Mexico and 100% hand-made with the lowest prices in the market.
www.impormexico.com

Bath & Body

Bath and body products have become a huge money maker for companies over the past few years. Companies selling their own versions of popular designer fragrances have also seen significant growth.

Bath products are great money makers as customer may buy various products of a favorite scent – bath gel, lotion and body spray for example. They also may pick up additional products for gifts, be repeat customers and refer others to you.

Lavare Bath & Body
Midwest company selling lotion bars, soaps, bath fizzies, bath salts, and more. 100% natural products and handmade fresh with every order.
www.lsbathcompany.com

Hodge Podge Corp
Hodge Podge Corp manufactures a large range of fine quality health & beauty products. Our clients range from retail, hotel and industrial to home based businesses; craft show exhibits and home party planners.
www.hodgepodgegifts.com

TC Laboratories
TC Labs specializes in the development of all natural and naturally-based skin care products, concentrates, additives and ingredients.
www.tclaboratories.com

Denham's Natural
Denham's Natural produces exclusive pure & natural body care products handmade to order within the United States at a price everyone can afford. We blend the very best of ingredients gathered from around the world to produce some of the finest pure skin care products available.
www.denhamsnatural.com

Bath & Body Continued

Boulder Bath and Body

Boulder Bath and Body products provide the foundation for healthy skin, therapeutic muscle recovery, respiratory performance, and emotional balance.
www.boulderbathandbody.com

Sonoma Aromas Bath & Body

Your one-stop spot for great bath, body and candle products. We will customize your favorite fragrance in a variety of lotions, soaps and bath products with candles to match.
www.sonomaaromas.com

Sweet Escence

Great bath and body products including bath gels, lotions, body sprays, massage oils, gifts sets, potpourri gel, and more.
www.sweetescence.com

Bath & Body Supply

Bath Body Supply is a wholesale bath and body suppliers for soap making bath body supplies and personal care toiletries dead sea salt and wholesale soap supply colorants.
www.bathbodysupply.com

Bath & Body Continued

Cosmetics, Skincare & Electronics Wholesale
1000s of high end department store brand name products up to 65% off MSRP!
www.fashiondivapalace.com

1st-perfume.com
We provide the public with access to the largest inventory of genuine, brand name fragrances and more at the lowest possible prices. We offer the best prices and availability for brand name perfumes, colognes, and body-care products.
www.1stperfume.com

Fragrance Factory
We are the manufacturers of the finest premium perfumes, fragrances, incense, and aromatherapy products available. Our incense is soaked and drenched in pure fragrance oils. Our perfumes contain no added alcohol and all of our fragrances are cosmetic grade so they can be worn on the skin.
www.fragrancefactory.com

Bath & Body Continued

Abbeys Perfume, LLC

We sell designer fragrances and perfumes. You can choose from women's perfume and fragrances, as well as men's perfume and fragrances such as Chanel, Estee Lauder, Gucci, Calvin Klein, Ralph Lauren and much more at wholesale prices
www.abbeysperfume.com

WholesaleBodyOils.com

The wholesale source for body oils, perfume oils, fragrance oils, bath and body products, bottles and supplies. Over 600 designer type and traditional fragrance oils, body oils, perfume oils and massage oils.
www.wholesalebodyoils.com

Luxury Perfumes Wholesale

22+ years wholesale/retail experience - 60 store locations worldwide. Over 10,000 designer wholesale fragrances, Hard to find, gift sets. 100% authentic, worldwide/international shipping, 24 hour orders. Trust our name and service at luxury perfumes. Watch our video on the about us page. 877 SCENT LA (723 6852)
www.luxuryperfume.com

Pet Supplies

You may have noticed more and more pet stores popping up in your area. That's because the pet industry is booming. Kiosks in malls feature nothing but pet items and flea market booths selling pet items often do well with repeat business and referrals.

King Wholesale Pet Supplies
King Wholesale pet supplies has been serving groomers, pet shops, veterinarians, kennels, trainers and breeders since 1987.
www.kingwholesale.com

Neeps Inc.
Neeps Inc. buys direct from over 60 leading manufacturers to ensure you are receiving the best price. And, unlike other distributors we never require a minimum order.
www.neeps-inc.com

RetailPets.com
RetailPets.com offers retailers quick and convenient access to the newest and most popular pet products.
www.retailpets.com

Royal Pet Supplies
Distributor of wholesale pet supplies (aquarium, bird, cat, dog, small animal) to the independent pet store.
www.royalpet.com

Marine Dog Leashes & Leads
Maker of Marine Dog and Marine Dog Junior dog products. Based in New York, established in 1999.
www.marinedog.com

Pet Supplies Continued

Pet Edge
Professional pet products and pet supplies for grooming, pet retailers, veterinarians, animal hospitals, boarding and kenneling and animal control.
www.petedge.com

Z-Fish Inc.
Z-Fish Inc. - Bringing you the best in pond plants, koi, tropical fish, reptiles and insects since 1965.
www.zfishinc.com

Ethnic & Historical

With the US seeing more and more people immigrating here, it is no wonder that people from different countries are looking for merchandise the same as or comparable to what they bought in their home country. These customers are often repeat buyers and will often refer family and friends.

On that same note, people are who get involved with historical re-enactments are often looking for detailed costumes and accessories. These people are often repeat buyers and will refer others in their groups and clubs.

Both of these areas are highly specialized and it is wise to educate yourself as much as possible about what you are selling.

Africa Imports
At Africa Imports we have searched and compiled the largest source of African products across the country. Over 1,500 African or African inspired items to choose from.
www.africaimports.info/index.asp

New York Trading Co
New York Trading Co - Your leading wholesaler of African Products.
www.africanproduct.com

Anadoli Collection
Anadoli Collection presents unique, handmade jewelry, gifts, home decor, collectibles, arts and crafts. This is where handcrafted gold, sterling silver, glass, ceramics, porcelain, mother of pearl and meerschaum meet art.
www.anadoli.com

Ethnic & Historical Continued

Wrights Peruvian Imports
We offer the best quality, handmade Peruvian jewelry at the most competitive prices. You will be pleased with the excellent value of our products as well as our prompt, courteous service.
www.peruvianjewelry.com

J R Palacios Enterprises
J R Palacios Enterprises has been in business since 1981. We have manufactured and distributed Western Products around the world since then.
www.jrpwesternproducts.com

Tombstone Outfitters
We are the oldest manufacturer of authentic western clothing and accessories in the world. We also offer a complete line of Civil War Uniforms and accoutrements.
www.tombstoneoutfitters.com

Ethnic & Historical Continued

Importaciones Mexico
Wholesale of German silver buckles, belts, wallets and western wear accessories. Our products are imported from Mexico and 100% hand-made with the lowest prices in the market.
www.impormexico.com

Navajo Shopping Center
The Navajo Shopping Center offers genuine sterling silver jewelry by Native American Indian Tribes, including Navajo, Zuni and Acoma.
www.navajoshop.com

El Paso Saddleblankets
Dealers and stores are needed to sell our fine hand-woven southwest design wool rugs, saddle blankets, wall hangings & saddle blankets.
www.elpasosaddleblanket.com

Sewing & Ribbons

Wedding and bridal professionals (as well as nonprofessionals) plus those who enjoy doing crafts are always looking for unusual ribbons as well as the best prices possible. Selling ribbons and various sewing supplies may often result in repeat business as well as referrals.

JKM Products
JKM Products Corporation has been in business over 9 years supplying Ribbon and Trims to the craft, bridal, floral, packaging, home sewing, design and specialty markets.
www.jkmribbon.com

M & J Trimming
Offering both wholesale and retail sales, M & J Trimming is a favorite shopping destination for the world's top fashion designers, costume makers, interior designers, and sewing and craft enthusiasts.
www.mjtrim.com

Self Defense & Security

The aftermath of 9/11 has resulted in people being more aware of their security. Our down economy has also caused crime to rise in some areas and people are becoming more and more aware of the need to protect themselves as some cities and towns are experiencing cutbacks. With this in mind, self- defense and security items are becoming increasingly popular. If you are selling at a flea market, you may wish to check with management regarding any policies they have in place about the sale of various items (as well as your local town or city) before purchasing any for re-sale.

TBO-Tech
Self-defense products such as stun guns, pepper sprays, tasers, knives and crossbows. As well as safety and security devices such as wireless home alarms, diversion safes, and child safety items.
www.tbotech.com

Safety Technology
Safety Technology has been wholesaling self-defense products since 1986, starting with one product - stun guns. Now we have hundreds of products available at wholesale prices.
www.safetytechnology.com

Security Plus Omni Corp
We are the prime source for Security Plus® brand of products consisting of pepper sprays, electronic stun guns, home, auto and personal alarms. We are also a factory authorized distributor of Mace®, AIR TASER® and Global Security™ products.
www.securitywholesaler.com

Self Defense & Security Continued

Cutting Edge Products
Manufacturer/Wholesaler of Streetwise Security Products including 900,000 volt stun guns, Pepper spray, alarms, can safes, and cameras. We sell wholesale, drop ship, and can even create a web site for you.
www.cuttingedgeproducts.net

A1 Security Products
We supply the self-defense needs of foreign civilians, foreign security personnel, police, military and government personnel with high quality products at fair prices.
www.militaryaction.org

Self Defense Supply
Self Defense Supply has the best quality items for you to purchase at discount prices. We continually strive to have to latest products available for you.
www.selfdefensesupply.com

Digital Watchguard
Digital Watchguard Inc. is your complete source for digital surveillance and IP based video security products. The most comprehensive catalog of digital surveillance equipment and accessories available to dealers, security professionals, and hobbyists.
www.digitalwatchguard.com

Self Defense & Security Continued

Alarm Systems Distributors
Wholesale burglar alarms from a distributor of security systems in Albany, New York, USA. Includes access control systems, burglar alarm equipment, CCTV security system equipment, fire alarm systems and IP cameras to retail stores.
www.alarmsystemsdist.com

CCTV Wholesale
American wholesale security merchandise company in Grover Beach, California. Specializing in CCTV security cameras, with CCTV accessories, camera mounts, lenses, security monitors, wires, cables, power supplies, multiplexors, infrared emitters, and complete CCTV security cameras available.
www.cctvwholesale.com

Digital Watchguard
USA based wholesale distributor offering security cameras, dome cameras, CCTV, DVR and IP network video cameras and products, based in Merrick, New York. We carry security cameras and accessories from major brands like Bosch, EverFocus, GeoVision, Samsung, GE Security, Fuji, AverMedia, Dedicated Micros, Nuvico, Vivotek and more.
www.digitalwatchguard.com

Safety Technology
Florida based drop ship wholesaler in the United States, of stun guns, pepper sprays, personal alarms, advanced tasers, diversion safes, voice changers and other self-defense products, hidden cameras, spy and surveillance systems.
www.safetytechnology.com

Self Defense & Security Continued

Securetek
American wholesale company based in Fort Lauderdale, Florida, selling digital surveillance and DVR specialist merchandise. Products include security cameras, dome security systems, CCTV, hidden security cameras, and bullet cameras. www.securetek.com

Skyline USA
Skyline offers wholesale personal security devices including stun guns, pepper spray, batons, air rifles, pistols and crossbows, located in Winter Springs, FL, USA. www.skylineusainc.com

Sunglasses

Sunglass sales have become a huge industry. More and more people are interested in buying them and with low prices people will often buy several pairs. While a small percentage of people used to wear sunglasses and mainly as a necessity, now they have become a fashion statement and are a great impulse item.

NYS Collection
Our product line is hands-down, the absolute BEST on the market. Our sunglasses are durable, provide maximum UV protection, and are, to say the least, very affordable.
www.nyscollection.com

Global Vision Eyewear
We are a wholesaler of quality sunglasses, goggles, safety glasses and accessories.
globalvision.us

Sunglasses Continued

Pacific Link Trade USA
Pacific Link Trade USA Inc. strives to manufacture and import quality eyewear with a wide assortment of designs to meet each individual's needs.
www.sunglassespacificlink.com

LA Sunglasses
We are a wholesaler and distributor of Sunglasses and Accessories. Call us for quantity discounts.
www.lasunglasses.com

Clip and Flip Eyewear
Clip and Flip Eyewear is a revolutionary new sports sunglasses design with 100% UV protection that incorporates a stylish wrap-around shield lens with its patented "Clip and Flip" nylon frame.
www.clipandflip.com

Sunglasses Continued

Sun Designe Ltd
Sun Designe Ltd is a wholesale distributor and importer of sunglasses and reading glasses.
www.sundesigne.com

Kachina LLC
Kachina is a manufacturer and wholesale distributor of sunglasses, fashion accessories and more.
www.kachinallc.com

LA Shades
LA Shades - bringing you quality DEZIGNER eyewear.
www.lashades.com

Sunglasses Continued

LA Wholesale Distributors
Our sunglasses are inspired by and comparable to the designer brand sunglasses.
www.lawholesaledist.com

Sunglass USA Inc.
Sunglass USA is a manufacturer, importer, exporter and wholesaler of fashion sunglasses.
www.sunglassusa.com

KW Sunglasses
KW Wholesale fashion Sunglasses. Top selling sunglasses for junior, vintage, unisex boutiques, dept., chain stores.
www.kwsunglasses.com

Sunny Trading Inc.
Sunny Trading Inc. is a direct importer and wholesaler of sunglasses.
www.sunico.com

Sunglasses Continued

Polar Ray
Great wholesale sunglass selection. Over 1000 styles, updated monthly, from promotional low cost line to upgrade quality lines.
www.polarray.com

Great L&H Trading
We offer hundreds of styles of quality sunglasses at competitive prices.
www.glhsunglasses.com

Survival Optics Sunglasses
Wholesale sunglasses manufacturer offering polarized sunglasses, goggles, sport sunglasses, golf sunglasses and motorcycle sunglasses.
www.soseyewear.com

Sunglasses Continued

The Fashion Group
The Fashion Group offers high quality, wholesale sunglasses with a distinct advantage, your Name and Logo. We offer custom sunglasses that are exclusively your product.
www.thefashiongroup.net

XS Sunglasses
We are the largest wholesaler of sunglasses on the internet. We only import and sell the highest of quality.
www.xs-sunglasses.com

Locs Sunglasses
BuyLocs.com is the top online retailer of Authentic Locs Sunglasses. We specialize in carrying the best Locs Sunglasses, Locs Shades and OG Locs Glasses.
www.buylocs.com

Sunglasses Continued

Miami Wholesale Sunglasses
Miami Wholesale Sunglasses is an online wholesaler of designer sunglasses. We offer over 400 wholesale designer sunglasses including DG Sunglasses, X-Loop Sunglasses, Locs Sunglasses and many others.
www.miamiwholesalesunglasses.com

D&G Sunglasses
DG Eyewear.com is the top online dealer of DG Sunglasses and Designer Sunglasses. We carry Discount Sunglasses at a Cheap Sunglasses price, All Under $30.
www.dgeyewear.com

Below Wholesale Sunglasses
Below Wholesale Sunglasses is the leader in sales and distribution of high quality wholesale sunglasses. We offer a 110% price-match guarantee on all of our styles.
www.belowwholesalesunglasses.com

Tools

Tools are always popular items to sell. From small to large items and everything in between a display of tools attracts potential buyers especially if the price is right.

Delancy Tool Corp

Wholesale and closeout hand tools and accessories.
www.delancytool.com

Mercantile Buyers Service

Your complete source for painting supplies: paint brushes, roller covers, roller frames, putty knives, wire brushes, extension poles, snap-off knives, dust masks, artist brushes, hand tools and other closeouts for all your paint and decorating needs.
www.mercantilebuyers.com

Wholesale Tool

Wholesale tool company headquartered in Warren, Michigan, USA. Offering a wide range of abrasives, air tools, automotive tools, carpentry tools, clamps, cutting tools, drill bits, educational material, electrical equipment, end mills, fluids, hand tools, hardware, machinery, maintenance equipment, material handling, power tools, precision equipment, pressure washers, safety equipment, sandblasters, setup tooling, vacuums, and welding equipment.
http://www.wttool.com

Tools Continued

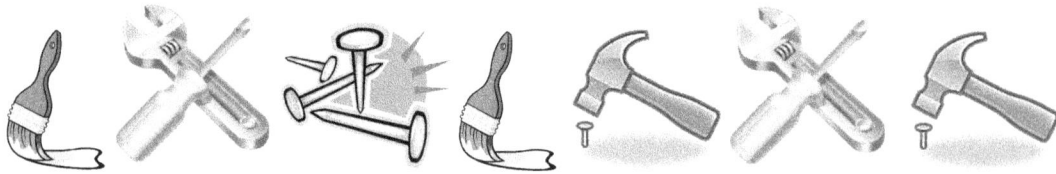

Bridgecraft USA

Bridgecraft offers a direct and reliable supply chain that brings you products from all over the world. We can help you bypass the middleman and buy directly from the importer of goods.

www.bridgecraftonline.com

Manufacturers Sales Co

Wholesale distributor of high performance industrial tools and accessories. Through distributors only.

www.msctools.com

Tools Continued

Merco Company
MercoTape.com - converter, manufacturer and importer of quality tape products, since 1972.
www.mercotape.com

Omaha Distributing Co
Importer of Omaha Tools, Omaha brand dollar store items, closeout merchandise wholesaler located in Omaha, Nebraska.
www.omahatool.com

Wiha Quality Tools
Manufacturers, exporter, supplier of hand tools from Germany.
www.wihatools.com

DP & Company
DP & Company Inc. is a Florida distributor of wholesale tools and general merchandise.
www.dpcompany.com

Tools Continued

A1 Wholesale Tools

American wholesale company in Omaha, NE with a tools by manufacturers that include Milwaukee, Bosch, DeWalt power tools, Skil, Makita, Wright Tool, Chicago Pneumatic, Ingersoll Rand, and Hitachi power tools. Also offering a range of woodworking machinery by Jet Equipment, Powermatic, Performax and Wilton.
http://www.a-1wholesaletool.com

Jchs Tools

USA tools wholesale company that dropships tools merchandise with offices in Pasadena, California, USA. Products available top dropship include garden tools, battery chargers, electric drills, car jacks, air tools, welders, grinders, shears, routers, tool sets, wrenches, spanners, pipe cutters, bandsaws, and tools from toolmakers and famous brands like Ryobi, Stanley, Makita, Skil, Dewalt, Corona, Milwaukee, and more.
http://www.jchstools.com

Manion's Wholesale

Wholesale building supplies company based in Superior, Wisconsin, USA. Manion's building supply company sells products to lumber yards and home centers located throughout Wisconsin, Minnesota, Michigan, North Dakota and South Dakota.
http://www.manionswholesale.com

Tools Continued

Tarps At Wholesale

Find wholesale tarps for covering hay, boats, gym floors, cars and building sites. Includes camouflage tarps, blue tarps, and fire retardant tarps.
http://www.tarpsatwholesale.com

Tri State Wholesale

American company based in Cincinnati, OH supplying building products to trades and industry. USA building supplies include doors, gutters, windows, railing, decking, screen enclosures, door accessories, marquee awnings, storm windows, window accessories and other products for the building trade.
http://www.tri-statewholesale.com

Wholesale Flashlights

American wholesale distributor of flashlights based in Blaine, Washington, U.S.A. Products include Maglite flashlights, Diamond shake lights, pen lights, key chain flashlights, Led flashlight bulbs, and more,
http://www.wholesale-flashlight.com

Beads

(Also see our Arts & Crafts listings)

Jewelry making is probably at an all - time high with people selling items online and on online sites such as Etsy. People who do beadwork are often looking for unusual beads as well as the standard staples.

Fire Mountain Gems
America's favorite beading and jewelry supply company. This company has been providing all sorts like Crystal Beads, Gemstone Beads, Glass Beads, Metal Beads, Natural Beads, Pearls, Acrylic Beads, Seed & Bugle Beads, Turquoise Beads. It has been established since 1973.
www.firemountaingems.com

Arizona Bead Company Inc.
wholesale supplier and importer of Swarovski Austrian Crystal Beads, Sterling silver and gold filled beads, Israeli silver, Czech glass beads, glass bead mixes, fiber optic (cat's eye) beads and fireball beads, magnetic hematite and magnetic clasps, stone beads, stringing wire, jewelry making tools, and much more.
www.arizonabeadcompany.com

Books

Despite the increase of e-books and internet use, books are still popular sellers. There are many options in selling books – selling books that are for a certain niche or selling a wide variety of overstocks and closeouts at a deep discount. The main thing is to create a display so that people can browse comfortably. A multi purchase discount also encourages people to buy more than one book.

American Book Co
American Book Company, one of the largest wholesale distributors of remainder, overstock, closeout, and bargain priced books.
www.americanbookco.com

Kudzu Book Traders
Kudzu Book Traders offers books below wholesale, overstocks, hurts and remainders.
www.kudzubooks.com

Bookliquidator.com
Our mission is to provide small retailers and book resellers a product that is profitable without requiring the customer to purchase high minimums orders or buy large quantities per title.
www.bookliquidator.com

Books Continued

Readers World USA
We are the nation's largest distributor of books to the independent marketer. With over 14 years' experience behind us, we have the buying power to allow the marketer to earn more money than they could anywhere else.
www.readersworldusa.com

Milligan News Co
Milligan News Company has been supplying books to schools, libraries, library programs, institutions, college stores, teachers and other educators since we established our school division in 1962.
www.milligannews.com

The Booksource | Classroom Libraries
Since 1974 The Booksource has been a family owned and operated national book wholesaler, distributing leveled books and children's book sets for classroom libraries.
www.booksource.com

Candles

Candles are most always a great traffic stopper. Long last fragrance is one reason most people select a certain brand as well as favorite scents. If you offer a quantity discount this also encourages people to buy more than just one. Repeat business can also be created as well as referrals from pleased customers. Consider including a free "gift" a book of matches with your company's information and also placing your contact info on the candle bottom with a nice sticker so if the candle is received as a gift the recipient will know where to buy more.

New York Candle
We are a family owned and operated company, manufacturing out of Staten Island. Our family has over forty years of fragrance & flavor development expertise, which has helped us in creating the strongest and most natural-like scented candles on the market.
www.newyorkcandle.com

Swan Creek Candle
Swan Creek Candle is a division of Ambrosia, Inc. an Ohio corporation that has been selling wholesale to the gift industry since 1978.
www.swancreekcandle.com

Southern Candle
Southern Candle Inc. is located at the base of the Blue Ridge Mountains of North Carolina in North Wilkesboro. The artistry and craftsmanship traditionally associated with Mountain people is evident in our outstanding line of scented jar candles.
www.southerncandle.com

Candles Continued

Unique Aromas
Unique Aromas, wholesale candles company, manufactures one of the largest selections of scented candles - gel candles, floating candles, pillars, votives, container candles, gift baskets and more.
www.candlescented.com

Keystone Products
Importer and Wholesaler of top quality incense and accessories from India. We import directly from the source to guarantee our products are always fresh.
www.keystoneproducts.com

Ruby Candle
Ruby Candle Company take great pride in our products. Each candle is hand poured to ensure top quality. As a family owned company, Ruby Candle Company pays special attention to all the details.
www.rubycandle.com

Acadian Candles
Acadian candles are individually handcrafted, using the highest grade of waxes, fragrances and dyes available.
www.acadiancandles.com

Candles Continued

Candlewic

CandleWic is your source for candle making and soap-making supplies, information and recipes. Our supplies and accessories include wholesale candle making kits, candle waxes, candle wicks, gels, molds, melt and pour bases, and soap dyes.
www.candlewic.com

Laura's Country Candles

Wholesale soy candles for sale on line at Laura's Country store. Clean burning, nontoxic, recyclable and environmentally friendly products.
www.laurascountrycandles.com

American Country

Jar candles and votives, hand poured in Maine. Available in 57 scents. Wholesale buyers can view and order online. Wholesale candles must be bought in cases. American-made candles in a variety of colors and scents. Votive assortments.
www.americancandlemakers.com

Creative Candles

Creative Candles - Every one of our candles is crafted by human hands and personal artistry.
www.creativecandles.com

Candles Continued

Mountain Candles
Specializes in scented candles, which are hand poured and dipped on the premises.
www.mountaincandles.com

General Wax & Candle
General Wax has been providing quality candles since 1949. Our origins are in institutional sales such as restaurants and churches. We pride ourselves in creating the best burning candles in the industry.
www.genwax.com

Applemill Cottage
Applemill Cottage sells retail, wholesale and private-label nationally and internationally. Dedicated to bringing you superior quality candle products.
www.applemillcottage.com

Unique Candles
Unique Candles has a selection of highly scented soy candles. Wholesale and private labeling also.
www.uniquecandles.net

Candles Continued

Crystal Journey Candles
Each of our candles are hand poured using the finest wax and an exotic blend of essential oils. The strong scent and colorful appearance of our candles are entrancing and your customers will be delighted.
www.crystaljourneycandles.com

Lizzie Candle
Our clean burning soy candles are scented in lovely muted colors or unscented in natural white soy wax. Our wholesale dealer section is now available for direct on line orders.
www.lizziecandles.com

Heritage Candles
Our high quality scented candles and fragrant jar candles are sold wholesale and retail and are a popular gift that appeals to a wide variety of customers.
www.heritagecandles.com

Déjà Vu Candles
Déjà Vu Candles is your resource for premium handmade candles and air freshener sprays. Our highly scented container candles and air freshener sprays feature the finest ingredients.
www.dejavucandles.com

Candles Continued

Prairie Candle

Prairie Candle Company is a family owned and operated business. At Prairie Candle Company we put quality first and foremost at all times. Our candles are hand poured using the highest quality wax and the finest fragrances.
www.prairiecandle.com

Avia Candles

Avia Candle Company makes quality scented candles for wholesale, retail and fundraising distributorships.
www.aviacandles.com

Wicks End Inc/Candles.com

Candle holders, oil lamps, pillar candles, unity candles, scented candles, taper candles, etc. We sell wholesale candles also.
www.candles.com

Gold Canyon Candle

Our incredible products, combined with our knowledgeable and dedicated distributors and demonstrators, have made us "The World's Finest"™ source for fragrant candles and accessories.
www.goldcanyoncandle.com

Candles Continued

Muffin Gems Candle Co
Offering highly scented primitive candles, candle fixings & refresher oils, rusty tin ware and other country primitive crafts. Wholesale inquiries welcome.
www.muffingems.com

Mrs. Candles
Premium hand poured candles triple scented. Many hard to find candle fragrances. Retail and wholesale candles.
www.mrs-candles.com

B&B Enterprises
Quality, hand-poured-to-order soy candles in exciting, collectable kitchenware. Choose your favorite scent and glassware. Gift baskets & certificates available.
www.scentsiblegift.com

Candles D-light
Offering a wide variety of dripless and smokeless taper candles, unscented long-burning votive candles, unscented pillars at discount and bulk discount prices.
www.dlightonline.com

Candy

Candy is not only a great impulse item but will bring repeat customers if you become known for selling certain brands, types or special candies such as sugar free ones that those who are diabetic can enjoy.

CandyXpress

Been in the wholesale candy business for over 63 years. Our company provides a full line of wholesale candy bars, chocolate candy, mints and hard candy, chewing gum, snacks, change makers bulk candy and other confectionery products.
www.candyxpress.com

Metro Candy & Nut

Metro Candy is your wholesale candy headquarters. Enjoy bulk candy and bulk chocolate delivered fast, right to your door at low wholesale prices. To keep our prices so low, our minimum order is $50 (excluding shipping).
www.metrocandy.com

MyCandySupplier.com

We offer a wide selection of candies, from new to nostalgia, many of which you probably remember enjoying as a kid and thought were no longer available.
www.mycandysupplier.com

Candy Favorites.com Online Candy Store

We are one of the oldest online candy stores backed by one of the oldest wholesale candy companies in the nation. We specialize in bulk candy, Brach's Candy and hard to find retro candies. Candy is what we deliver but service is what we sell.
www.candyfavorites.com

Candy Continued

Sugar Man Candy
Sugar Man Candy is your wholesale candy headquarters for rock candy, lollipops, gumballs and more.
www.sugaramancandywholesale.com

Candy Direct
The oldest candy store on the Internet. We offer a wide selection of candies, from new to nostalgia, many of which you probably remember enjoying as a kid and thought were no longer available.
www.candydirect.com

Albanese Confectionery
The world's largest maker of Gummie candies. Tours are available.
www.albaneseconfectionery.com

Old Time Candy Co.
Candy you ate as a kid®. We have Fizzies, Wax Lips, Licorice Snaps, Kits, Wax Bottles, Candy Cigarettes, Necco Wafers, Candy Buttons on paper tape, Sky Bars, Atomic Fireballs, Satellite Wafers, BB Bats, Bubble Gum Cigars, Now & Laters and much more fresh old fashioned candy from the 50s, 60s, 70s and 80s.
www.oldtimecandy.com

Phones and Accessories

People are always looking for good prices and deals on phones and accessories. Often name brand accessories are very costly in traditional retail stores. Developing a reputation of offering quality phones and phone accessories at a great price will help bring in repeat business

EBK Manufacturing
We're an established wholesale cellular phone supplier in the Midwest with large inventories, quality products, excellent service and product warranties.
www.ebkmfg.com

ReCellular
ReCellular is a world leader in buying and selling used cell phones in bulk. We carry all brands and technologies, as well as accessories and other types of refurbished wireless equipment.
www.recellular.net/home/home.asp

Lewis Wireless
Used cell phones for dealers, and vendors selling at swaps meets, flea markets, festivals, fairs and fund raising events.
www.lewiswireless.com

Phones and Accessories Continued

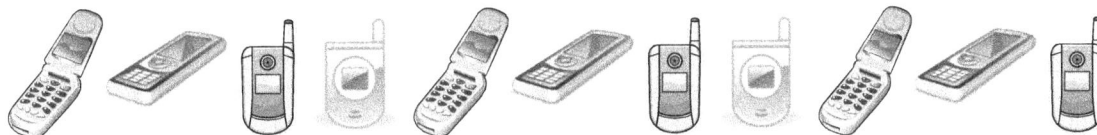

Wireless Emporium
Wholesale prices on mobile phone accessories.
www.wirelessemporium.com

My Cool Cell
My Cool Cell stocks all the latest phone accessories at deep discount wholesale.
www.mycoolcell.net

Cellular Outfitter
If you're looking for cheap prices and wholesale deals, contact us.
www.cellularoutfitter.com

Closeouts & Liquidation Merchandise

Closeouts and liquidation packages are readily available in a variety of price ranges. Check regarding actual freight charges to your area and if the company is located nearby see if you can pick up the merchandise. Packages such as these are great in that you have a large variety of merchandise to sale. Be sure to do your research before agreeing to buy. Find out if the merchandise is new, damaged, salvage, broken etc. before you place your order.

Libra Inc.
Closeouts have made LIBRA an innovative wholesaler of brand name merchandise, with an emphasis on USA made closeouts.
www.librausa.com

Quality Closeouts
Founded in 1982, GRQC buys and sells deeply discounted merchandise for the discount retail industries.
www.qualitycloseouts.com

Division Sales
Division Sales offers more than wholesale dollar merchandise; we are dollar specialists who know how to move merchandise. At Division Sales you'll find exciting closeouts, plus new items from around the world.
www.divisionsales.com

Rhinomart
Rhinomart specializes in the wholesale of department store returns, customer returns, liquidation merchandise, & salvage pallets/truckloads.
www.rhinomart.com

Closeouts & Liquidation Merchandise Continued

Big Lots Wholesale
Big Lots Wholesale.com is a business-to-business exchange that provides top-quality merchandise at below-wholesale prices.
www.biglotswholesale.com

TDW Closeouts
Closeouts overstock worldwide distributor and export of Department Store Returns and Closeout Merchandise, offering closeouts, liquidation merchandise, salvage, surplus, and a whole lot more at pennies on the wholesale dollar.
www.tdwcloseouts.com

Jack Levy Sales
Since 1975, Jack Levy Sales has been a leading name in closeout general merchandise. We specialize in giftware, house wares, collectables, novelties, and licensed items.
www.jacklevysales.com

RLC Trading
RLC Trading specializes in the distribution of closeout & surplus clothing. We supply Discount Outlets, Closeout Stores, Auction Sellers, Flea Market Vendors and On-line Stores with wholesale name brand inventory.
www.rlctrading.com

Closeouts & Liquidation Merchandise Continued

Kristie's Deals
Kristie's Closeouts, the best in closeout merchandise! Kristie's is widely recognized as being tops in the closeout industry. We sell top quality, name brand merchandise to individuals as well as dealers.
www.kristiesdeals.net

Countryside Closeouts
The best in name brand closeouts you can find. Countryside Closeouts has a large selection of low cost merchandise.
www.countryside-closeouts.com

HJ Liquidators
H and J Liquidators and Closeouts are in the wholesale closeout, surplus, liquidation business where they buy and sell almost anything at a price way below wholesale.
www.surplus.net/hj

United Discount
Our Company has been in business since 1983, we specialize in close out discontinued and overstock Items we also own US Comfort brand products that we sell.
www.uniteddiscount.com

Closeouts & Liquidation Merchandise Continued

Roden Surplus Imports
Rodenimports.com offers a wide variety of wholesale closeouts at way below wholesale pricing. We have thousands of items with new arrivals daily.
www.rodenimports.com

Great Discounters
Great Discounters specializes in the purchasing of excess inventories, liquidations and bankruptcy merchandise.
www.greatdiscounters.com

US Liquidation
We are one of the leading liquidators of Major Department Stores Overstocked, Surplus, Closeout, Damaged, and Customer Returned Inventories.
www.usliquidation.com

USA Overstock
Overstock Liquidation Merchandise and Closeouts Surplus Merchandise.
www.usaoverstock.com

Closeouts & Liquidation Merchandise Continued

My Bargain Bin LLC
We specialize in wholesale, liquidation and closeout merchandise. We sell, wholesale body art, beauty products, hair accessories, glow lites and novelties.
www.mybargainbin.com

Jane's Closeout Marketplace
Negotiate online with our wholesale suppliers for overstock merchandise at discounted wholesale prices. Features order processing, tracking and free escrow services.
www.janesdeals.com

Liquidation.com
Manufacturers, retailers and wholesalers convert surplus assets into cash using our online auctions and integrated services. Professional buyers benefit from our fast and secure method to source surplus.
www.liquidation.com

Closeouts & Liquidation Merchandise Continued

Bargain Warehouse
New and returned merchandise, sold by the pallet or truckload. Direct from major department stores. Electronics, housewares, HBA, apparel, sports.
www.thebargainwarehouse.com

Closeouts Concepts
Americas Closeouts Specialist. We are the primary supplier of liquidation, salvage, overstock and closeout merchandise. We sell by the lot, pallet, truckload and container. Buy direct from Closeouts Concepts and save all the intermediate costs.
www.closeoutsconcepts.com

BulkWorks Inc.
Whether you're a small business or a large corporation, if you want to expand your reach and sell your products through more retail stores, mail-order catalogs, and Internet shopping sites.
www.bulkworks.com

Pick-A-Part LLC
We are a mass wholesalers in business for over 30 years. We work with odd lots, job lots, liquidations, orphans, buybacks, closeouts, package hanging, surplus, changeovers; lift outs, obsolete items, and much more.
www.pikapart.com

Closeouts & Liquidation Merchandise Continued

Farah Trading
We are a worldwide distributor and exporter of electronics and general merchandise. We handle new, used, refurbished, customer returned, salvaged, surplus, closeouts and overstocked inventory.
www.liquidatedelectronics.com

Chicago Liquidation
Over 100 truckloads of merchandise in our warehouse always.
www.chicagoliquidation.com

West Coast Trading
West Coast Trading is a complete wholesaler & outlet specializing in the sale of all name brands. We do business with America's ten largest major department stores.
www.westcoasttrading.com

Shasta Liquidations
Hundreds of liquidation products including apparel, health & beauty, toys, sports, home & garden and more at prices way below wholesale. Perfect for E-bayers, Flea Marketers and retail storefronts.
www.wholesalecentral.com/giftex0001/store.cfm

Closeouts & Liquidation Merchandise Continued

Mid-America Liquidators
Your #1 wholesale distributor in excess inventory, offering you saving solutions on closeout merchandise, overstock merchandise, customer return loads and surplus inventory.
www.midamliq.com

Merchandise USA
Merchandise USA Inc. is a wholesale merchandise closeout company in business 20 years.
www.merchandiseusa.com

Atlas Traders
The shopping center for quality discount clothing, electronics and discount products below wholesale and surplus, overstock and overrun products such as discount clothing.
www.atlastraders.com

Closeouts & Liquidation Merchandise Continued

World Liquidators
Store returns, store closeouts, major department stores - World Liquidators - the #1 Supplier in the US.
www.worldliquidators.net

Bilco & Associates
Bilco was founded in the spring of 1977 to provide quality closeouts and premiums to all types of companies.
www.bilcoonline.com

Boswell Trade Center
Boswell Trade Center is a Wholesale Dealer Auction located in Boswell, Indiana. Boswell Trade Center is a new concept in the sale and distribution of closeouts.
www.closeout-auction.com

Closeouts & Liquidation Merchandise Continued

Sav-on-Closeouts

We currently have about 1,000 closeout offers with new merchandise arriving every week. No membership or other fees. No minimum order.
www.sav-on-closeouts.com

Bargain Liquidators

Our goal is to skip all third parties and brokers, cutting commissions, to bring you better priced deals and better services in our most efficient way, providing you with great liquidation bargains.
www.bargainliquidators.com

Topper International

Topper International Liquidators are your closeout specialists. We provide quality closeouts at prices far below wholesale.
www.topper.com

Worldwide Liquidators

Worldwide Liquidators LLC - We have been in the closeout business for over ten years, and continually strive to sell great products at great prices.
www.wwliquidators.com

Closeouts & Liquidation Merchandise Continued

O'Shea Ltd
We buy manufacturers closeouts so you get great savings. See the world smallest fax in our closeout site.
www.oshealtd.com

My Web Wholesaler
Wholesale liquidation, surplus, merchandise closeouts, overstock and shelf pulls: Jewelry, electronics, clothing, toys and more. No minimum order requirements.
www.mywebwholesaler.com

Gibraltar Wholesale
With over 20 years in the Closeout business, Gibraltar Wholesale has the experience to handle and size order placed or inventory offered for sale. Wholesale, closeouts and liquidations are our specialty.
www.gtcwholesale.com/store

Closeouts & Liquidation Merchandise Continued

Closeout Services Corp
We sell closeout merchandise at the most competitive prices, from toys & novelties to licensed products; premiums & promotions to hats & tees.
www.closeoutservices.com

AAA Closeouts Network
Specializes in closeouts, liquidations, bulk wholesale, surplus, salvage, overstocks, cancellations and store returns.
www.aaacloseoutsnetwork.com

American Merchandise Group
American Merchandise Group is one of the fastest growing promotional products companies in the country. We specialize in the Sales and Purchasing of closeouts, overstock, takedowns and obsolete products.
www.amgcorp.net

Southern Tool Supply
We have perfected a system that is capable of handling multi-store shipments of buybacks as well as factory buyouts.
www.southerntoolsupply.com

Closeouts & Liquidation Merchandise Continued

Cricket Hill Liquidators

Cricket Hill is always interested in establishing new relationships with individuals or companies engaged in the business of distressed merchandise disposition.
www.crickethillliquidators.com

Closeout Solution

CloseOutSolution.com – Your solution to purchasing name brands at clearance prices.
www.closeoutsolution.com

Redemption Enterprises

We are a retail and wholesale company that carries name brand merchandise at a fraction of wholesale. We specialize in purchasing bankruptcies, unclaimed freight, insurance claims, and all closeout merchandise.
www.redemptionenterprises.com

Closeouts & Liquidation Merchandise Continued

Brand Name Liquidators
Carpet, rugs and vinyl flooring from Dalton, Ga. Drugstore and household merchandise closeouts.
www.savehere.com

Ninos Trading
Best supplier of customer returns, liquidations, store displays, shelf items, closeouts, factory refurbished and salvage merchandise by the pallet, lot or truckload.
www.ninostrading.com

Jacobs Trading Co
We only sell by the truckload to a variety of outlets including: discount and surplus stores; flea market vendors; auctioneers; and on-line wholesalers and retailers.
www.jacobstrading.com

Prako Inc.
Prako is a trusted resource for buying and selling customer returned and excess merchandise.
www.prako.com

Closeouts & Liquidation Merchandise Continued

American Merchandise Liquidators

American Merchandise Liquidators Inc. is a solid bricks-and-mortar, ten-year plus company, contracted and trusted nationwide to move millions in distressed merchandise.
www.amlinc.com

Allstate Liquidation

Allstate Liquidation is a large-scale dealer of overstock, return and surplus apparel to markets large and small.
www.allstateliquidation.com

Discount Wholesalers

Discount Wholesalers Inc. specializes in the wholesale of overstock, customer returns, liquidation merchandise, closeouts (pallets/truckloads).
www.1dwi.com

Liquidation Connection

Liquidation Connection provides a solution to manufacturers and importers to sell large and small quantities of discontinued, closeout merchandise at higher prices than normally received from traditional liquidators.
www.liquidationconnection.com

Closeouts & Liquidation Merchandise Continued

DRC Distributors
Closeouts in power tools accessories, sanding belts & other abrasives and Dremel® type items. Most closeouts priced at half of distributors pricing.
www.drcdist.com

Monster Closeouts
Closeouts, Retail Overstock, Liquidation Merchandise, Surplus Goods and Department Store Returns by the pallet, lot and truckload at pennies on the wholesale dollar.
www.monstercloseouts.net

DJH Inc.
Name Brand Closeout Specialists. We are the leaders in all kinds of general merchandise closeouts.
www.djhinc.com

A & W Surplus
A & W Surplus is the place to find high quality wholesale and closeout merchandise such as electronics, car audio, home entertainment and general merchandise at incredible prices. Buy by the pallet, box, lot or come to our auctions.
www.awsurplus.com

Closeouts & Liquidation Merchandise Continued

Pallets Mart

PalletsMart carries a full line of salvage merchandise, closeouts merchandise, surplus closeouts, department stores closeouts, department store returns and salvage truckload cosmetics from the top department stores in America.
www.palletsmart.com

Oceanis Inc.

Oceanis Inc. is a wholesaler, importer and closeout buyer of value oriented dollar and variety store merchandise.
www.oceanisinc.com

CloseoutsUSA.com

CloseoutsUSA.com is in business to bring its customers the best quality merchandise at the best possible price. We buy direct from major manufacturers and pass the savings along to you.
www.closeouts-usa.com

Value Supply LLC

Value Supply is a source for wholesale closeouts overstocks and discontinued products.
www.vsmerchandise.com

Closeouts & Liquidation Merchandise Continued

Closeouts Trading.com
We are your leading supplier and distributor of wholesale, salvage, surplus, discontinued or distressed merchandise, brand names, department store shelf pulls & returns, closeouts, liquidation, overstock, stock lots, lot goods, factory overruns, buybacks, seconds & irregulars.
www.closeoutstrading.com

Surplus Giant
Surplus Giant Inc. is a wholesale-liquidation distributor. SGI specializes in closeout products, excess and surplus inventories.
www.surplusgiant.com

Warehouse One
At Warehouse One we wholesale store returns, surplus, overstocks, salvage, liquidations, shelf pulls, and closeouts.
www.warehouseone.net

BuyMe.Net
BuyMe.Net is an online wholesale liquidator of office equipment, consumer electronics, networking products, computer peripherals, household products, and more.
www.buyme.net

Closeouts & Liquidation Merchandise Continued

Liquidation Treasures
LiquidationTreasures.com carries the finest jewelry liquidation and jewelry closeout products in the net.
www.liquidationtreasures.com

Harry J Epstein Co
Closeout American made hand tools and general merchandise. We buy tool closeouts, liquidations, overstocks and offer them at below manufacturers cost.
www.harryepstein.com

Chicago Liquidation Distributors
Chicago Liquidation Distributors is a worldwide distributor and exporter of department stores liquidation, store returns and closeout merchandise, offering the absolute best closeouts, liquidation items, salvage stock, overstocks and surplus merchandise products.
www.liquidationdistributors.com

Closeouts & Liquidation Merchandise Continued

Triangle Marketing
Triangle Marketing Inc. is a wholesale organization trading in closeout merchandise since 1975.
www.tmicloseouts.com

RS Trading
Closeouts and liquidation merchandise, offering overstock, customer returns, surplus merchandise, and salvage goods.
www.rstrading.com

Atlantic Surplus
Atlantic Surplus sells wholesale shoes; wholesale Rhino work boots, wholesale jeans, wholesale handbags, wholesale clothing, used jeans, used Levi jeans, used clothing, used shoes, used toys, used baseball caps, used handbags, and miscellaneous closeout, surplus, and overstock merchandise.
www.atlanticsurplus.com

Coffee

Coffee's popularity has exploded the past few years. More and more people are trying different flavors and grinds as well as buying accessories. Socially responsible options are also gaining in popularity. Coffee also is a great addition to gift bags and baskets.

Espresso Zone
Espresso Zone specializes in gourmet products and supplies for the coffee enthusiast. Since inception in 2000 we have established a solid reputation in the coffee community, serving thousands of satisfied customers throughout the United States.
www.espressozone.com

Stone Creek Coffee
We have worked hard to create not only amazing coffee but also strong company processes to make doing business with us easy and clear. Our coffees are recognized as among the best in our market, our service is reliable and fast, and our marketing is active and creative.
sccv3.stonecreekcoffee.com

Jeremiah's Pick Coffee Co.
A specialty roaster committed to supplying the highest quality fresh-roasted coffee to fine food, high-end grocery stores, premier restaurants and hotels on the West Coast.
www.jeremiahspick.com

Momentto Coffee Roasting Co
Momentto Coffee Roasting Co. specialized in Ethnic coffee products like Turkish-Greek coffee. Offering Minas Gold coffee.
www.momenttocaffe.com

Coffee Continued

Grounds For Change
Fair trade, organic, shade grown coffees. Our coffees are recognized as among the best in our market. We provide fast and reliable service.
www.groundsforchange.com

Coffee and Tea Warehouse
100% Arabica beans with wholesale options available.
www.coffeeandteawarehouse.com

Ecosense Coffees
Anyone can order. Wholesale pricing available. Eco-sustainable coffees from around the world. Free private labeling.
www.ecosensecoffees.com

Collectibles, Comic Books & Sports Memorabilia

People who collect items such as comic books, sports memorabilia and other collectibles often are well versed in what items are worth. They also will often search relentlessly for a certain item in a certain condition. If you can brand yourself as the "go to guy" for hard to find merchandise, you may see steady growth and repeat customers. This is an area that may require reading trade publications and attending various trade shows but it is also an area that may be a very profitable money maker.

Diamond Comic Distributors
Diamond Comic Distributors, Inc. was established in 1982 to provide comic book specialty retailers with wholesale, non-returnable comic books and related merchandise.
www.diamondcomics.com

M &J Variety Distributors
Retail and Wholesale Toys and collectibles. Online Store, Mail order, Phone orders, and Auctions.
www.mjvar.com

Pittsburgh Sports Wholesale
Pittsburgh Sports Wholesale - Baseball cards, Prices Updated Daily. Over 1,000 unopened boxes and packs from all 4 major sports available. We also carry unopened boxes of Racing, Golf, Yugioh and a complete line of sports card supplies.
www.pghsportswholesale.com

Collectibles, Comic Books & Sports Memorabilia Continued

Edgeman.com
Your online source for sports, non-sports, collectible card games and more.
www.edgeman.com

Jason's Wholesale
Our company has been in business for over twenty years selling toys and general merchandise to a variety of wholesale accounts. We have been serving the retail and wholesale marketplace via the World Wide Web since 1998.
www.jasonswholesale.com

Baseline Sports
Baseline Sports is premium wholesale distributer for all sorts of sports memorabilia and supplies. We deal in major brands such as Topps, Pinnacle Brands, Don Russ Trading Card and Upper Deck.
www.blsports.com

Michael Trading Group
Michael Trading Group is a wholesaler of gifts, closeouts, collectibles and licensed merchandise.
www.michaeltrading.com

Sports Line Distributors
Sports Line Distributors has been the #1 choice of retailers for over 15 years. Our extensive product lines include sports cards, gaming cards, bobble heads and action figures, die-cast vehicles and a large variety of licensed sports products.
www.sportslined.com

Collectibles, Comic Books & Sports Memorabilia Continued

Kool Collectibles
We manufacture and wholesale the finest Nostalgic Decor.
www.koolcollectibles.com

Mid-South Products
Mid-South Products is your one stop Nostalgia Dealer.
www.midsouthproducts.com

Classic Sports Distributors
Classic Sports Distributors Inc. is the retailer's choice for officially licensed wholesale sports and Olympic pins and accessories.
www.classicpins.net

Casey's Distributing
Casey's has a wide selection of over 2,000 products that are in stock and ready for shipment.
www.caseys-distributing.com

Hometown Collectibles
We're a small US company dedicated to creating products that reflect and support the pride that people feel for their own hometowns - and for their nation.
www.hometowncollectibles.com

Collectibles, Comic Books & Sports Memorabilia Continued

Harbour Lights
Harbour Lights - Award winning collectible Light Houses.
www.harbourlights.com

Smiles Wholesale
In business since 1996, our mission is to provide you with some of the finest deals to be found anywhere on the web! We are very excited about expanding our business to the web and sharing our incredible deals with the online wholesale buyer.
www.smileswholesale.com

General Merchandise

General merchandise priced right may attract a steady flow of repeat customers and referrals. If you are stocking everyday items priced right, it's easy for someone to plan on stocking up when they come to your store.

Concord Enterprises
The web's leading source of dollar store item merchandise, 99 cent store item and over $1 dollar general item merchandise, wholesale importer.
www.concordent.com

Dollar Days International
Dollar Days is the premiere online wholesaler and closeout company that helps small businesses to compete against larger enterprises by offering more than 25,000 high-quality goods at prices close to those at which large chains purchase.
www.dollardays.com

Glaze Inc.
Founded Over 15 Years Ago And Dedicated To Finding Products That Are In Demand. Our Goal Is To Provide Products To Our Customers With Exceptional Value, Quality, Fast Service And Most Of All, Reliability.
www.glazeinc.com

General Merchandise Continued

B&F System
B & F System sells wholesale to businesses and marketing professionals.
www.bnfusa.com

Bargain Supply Co
We have been doing business in the original location since 1950. Offering great prices on a variety of general merchandise and providing our customers with fast, friendly service.
www.bargain-mall.com/store

World Distributors
Online catalog with more than 3,000 different items. Visit us for a free catalog.
www.worlddist.com

General Merchandise Continued

Pioneer Trading Co
Established in 1976 to distribute quality products to small business and swap meet vendors around the country.
www.tradeatpioneer.com

Bethel International
We are a diversified wholesale company providing retailers a broad range of merchandise to retail stores all across the United States.
www.bethelwholesale.com

Sasser Distributing
Sasser Distributing Company is your complete online wholesale outlet.
www.sasserdistributing.com

STK International
Wholesale importers of general merchandise for 99 cents stores. Distributor for retail outlets. We do direct imports.
www.stkinternational.com

General Merchandise Continued

Navajo Manufacturing
Navajo Manufacturing Company is a wholesale supplier of non-food products for C-stores and other retail store outlets.
www.navajomfg.com

Dollar Store Source
We are a full service company providing General Merchandise, Specialty Items, Giftware and Seasonal Items for your everyday needs.
www.dollarstoresource.com

Eagle Distributors
Eagle Distributors Inc. is a reputable supplier to major clienteles in the fields of cash-n-carry, wholesalers, chain grocers, mass merchandisers and volume buyers among many others.
www.eagledistinc.com/index2.htm

General Merchandise Continued

Slam Bam Fun Merchandise
Slam Bam Fun Merchandise is a stock house supplying over 2,500 items made in the USA, Hong Kong, China, Taiwan, Korea, Canada and Mexico.
www.slambamfun.com

Mazer Wholesale
We are an importer and wholesale distributor of plastic housewares, general merchandise, hand tools, painting tools, hardware, brooms and other cleaning items and items in many other categories.
www.mazerwholesale.com

Regent Products
Regent Products Corp is a leader in the close-out and merchandising industry. Since 1985, we've been meeting our goal of providing retailers and wholesalers with consistent service and exceptional value.
www.regentproducts.com

General Merchandise Continued

Wholesale Imports

We sell wholesale costume jewelry, beauty supplies, fashion accessories, giftware and general merchandise.
www.wholesaleimport.com

Kassir Co Inc.

Your one stop shop for best-selling merchandises at the best prices. We are distributors to almost all consumers varying from Wholesaler, Retailer, Mini Mart, Chain Store, Convenient Store, Liquor Store, Dollar Store, Gas Station Mart, 99 cent Store and Jobber Market for more than 12 years.
www.kassirco.com

Rust Wholesale

Rust Wholesale Company is a full service variety and craft distributor serving retail merchants in a 48-state area.
www.rustwholesale.com

General Merchandise Continued

Mita Inc.
In business since 1995. We carry all major brand leather goods, watches, small electronics, caps, T-shirts and more at low price.
www.mitainc.com

Global Time
Manufacturer, importer and wholesale distributor of watches, electronics & novelties.
www.globaltimeintl.com

BOZZ USA
BOZZ USA is the country's leading importer, exporter, wholesaler, distributor of electronics and consumer products. We are known for our high quality, standards, durability, and great prices.
www.bozzusa.com

General Merchandise Continued

Direct Source Imports Wholesale
Direct Source Imports is a nationally known manufacturer and wholesaler of business & premium gifts, cookware, knives, incentive merchandise and advertising specialties.
www.BuyDsi.com

Kole Imports
Dollar store, 99 cent store items and over $1 general merchandise. Wholesale Importer. Kole Imports is your dollar store specialist.
www.koleimports.com

Furad Wholesale
We have thousands of wholesale products at everyday low prices. You can find anything from housewares to baby items and everything in between.
www.furad.com

Elbin International
We are an established provider of full service import / export solutions. Since 1977 we have provided assistance in all aspects of the global product market including design, production, and imports-exports.
www.elbin.com

General Merchandise Continued

Westbury Sales
Wholesale dollar store supplier, discount general merchandise and dollar store wholesale supplier.
www.westburysales.com

Surplus City Wholesale
Wholesale Distributor Dealing In Closeouts and Below Wholesale merchandise dealer in closeouts, wholesale, bargains, deals for retail, dollar, gift and flea market sales.
www.scwholesale.com

Direct Source Imports Wholesale
Direct Source Imports is a nationally known manufacturer and wholesaler of business & premium gifts, cookware, knives, incentive merchandise and advertising specialties.
www.BuyDsi.com

General Merchandise Continued

Kole Imports
Dollar store, 99 cent store items and over $1 general merchandise. Wholesale Importer. Kole Imports is your dollar store specialist.
www.koleimports.com

Furad Wholesale
We have thousands of wholesale products at everyday low prices. You can find anything from housewares to baby items and everything in between.
www.furad.com

Global Time
Manufacturer, Importer and Wholesale Distributor of Watches, Electronics & Novelties.
www.globaltimeintl.com

General Merchandise Continued

BOZZ USA
BOZZ USA is the country's leading importer, exporter, wholesaler, distributor of electronics and consumer products for its highest quality, standards, durability, and great prices.
www.bozzusa.com

Elbin International
We are an established provider of full service import / export solutions. Since 1977 we have provided assistance in all aspects of the global product market including design, production, and imports-exports.
www.elbin.com

General Merchandise Continued

STW Merchandising

Family owned and operated wholesale company that has an "old fashioned" value – in that serving the customer is the reason we are in business.
www.stw-wholesale.com/store.cfm

7 Elephants Distributing

7Elephants Imports distributes and exports car audio (speakers, amplifiers, cd players tweeters, subwoofer, crossovers, car lcd monitors), jackets (leather, PVC, sport) watches, cameras, blankets, perfumes, colognes, hair clippers, boots, and more.
www.7elephants.com

JD Yeatts

We import thousands of quality items from all over the world. We sell exclusively to qualified dealers. Our products range from lawn & garden, candles, toys, giftware, seasonal items, closeouts, hammocks, hardware, housewares and more.
www.jdyeatts.com

General Merchandise Continued

Westbury Sales
Wholesale Dollar Store Supplier Discount General Merchandise and Dollar Store Wholesale Supplier.
www.westburysales.com

Surplus City Wholesale
Wholesale distributor dealing in closeouts and below wholesale merchandise. Your top dealer source for closeouts, wholesale, bargains, deals for retail, dollar items, gifts and flea market sales.
www.scwholesale.com

KCP Wholesale
Wholesale distribution company specializing in name brand cosmetics such as L'Oreal, Lancôme, Maybelline, Revlon. Also designer alternative eyewear/sport goggles, high fashion jewelry, general merchandise, closeouts and much more.
www.kcpwholesale.com

General Merchandise Continued

National Distributors
Wholesale merchandising company offering many categories by Catalog to Hospital Gift Shops, Hotels & Resorts, Pharmacies, Casinos, Camping Facilities, Travel Plazas and Correctional Institutions located in all 50 United States.
www.nationaldistributors.com

Brookland Sales Inc.
Brookland Sales is the wholesale distributor retailers have turned to for two generations! Our selection of quality merchandise includes silk flowers, greenery, cast iron, giftware, dolls, knick-knacks, hardware, hand tools, swords, knives, and much more.
www.brooklandsales.com

TCB Imports
TCB Imports is a specialized company in manufacturing and importing general merchandise. Our price competitiveness offers great buying opportunities for all our customers ranging from dollar stores to discount chain stores.
www.tcbimports.com

General Merchandise Continued

Dromar Inc.
Dromar Inc. - Wholesale Souvenirs and Gifts.
www.dromar.com

Apex Merchandising
Apex Merchandising Group Inc. offers great deals on thousands of dollar store items. We carry toys, tools, hardware, house wares, phone & cable accessories, pet, health and beauty, bandanas, novelty, key chains, plastics, stationery, and much more.
www.apexmerchandise.com

Axiom International
We are an importer of general merchandise. Our products range from sunglasses/reading glasses, toys, party supplies, balloons, and incense.
www.axiomintl.com

General Merchandise Continued

Pride Products
Pride Products has been in business for 20 years. We distribute over 4,000 imported and domestic products in over 100 different categories.
www.prideproducts.com

Pricemaster Corp
PriceMaster - Your Number One distributor of electronics and general merchandise with over 1,000 items.
www.pricemaster.com

Price King Inc.
Price King is a leading wholesaler selling mainly to $1 stores, variety stores, photo stores, drug stores and others.
www.priceking.com

Acme Sales
Importers, Wholesalers & Distributors of General Merchandise Since 1927.
www.acmesales1927.com

General Merchandise Continued

Value King Wholesale

We carry candy, cigarettes, stationary, film, batteries, school supplies, paper goods, cigars, novelty items, audio/video cassettes, health and beauty items, general merchandise much more.
www.valuekingwholesale.com

K&R Wholesale

K&R Wholesale sells exclusively to C-store distributors, C-store wholesalers, novelty distributors and grocery wholesalers.
www.krwholesaleinc.com

ENOR International

ENOR International specializes in the design, importation and distribution of all types of butane gas refillable and disposable lighters. We offer our products in the most unique and the most innovative displays for quick high impulse sales.
www.enorusa.com

General Merchandise Continued

MainWholesaler.com
We offer a wide variety of brand name convenience-store products. We are a one-stop shop for customers (with verifiable tax-id's) who service and supply the convenience store market.
www.mainwholesaler.com

LA Lighter
As the premier product in cigarette lighters worldwide LA Lighter manufactures and markets the widest spectrum of lighters delivery systems today.
www.lalighter.com

Corban Exchange
Corban Exchange offers drop ship wholesale service for the hottest products on eBay with exclusive agreements with eBay's best sellers.
www.corbanexchange.com

General Merchandise Continued

RFK Associates
RFK Associates is a 44 year old company specializing in the sale of Duracell and Eveready batteries as well as Polaroid and Kodak film.
www.rfkassociates.com

MCT Wholesale
MCT Wholesale is a wholesale distributor delivering full service and a comprehensive line of products to convenience stores, tobacco shops and the petroleum industry in Georgia.
www.mctweb.com

NBSP Inc.
NBSP Inc. are importers of high quality general merchandise, health and beauty aids and novelty items.
www.nbspinc.com/home/home.html

A&J Distributing Corp
Wholesaler that provides premier delivery and pricing of products to convenience stores nationwide. Our range of products is large and diversified to help provide the items your customers need.
www.anjdistributing.com

General Merchandise Continued

STW Merchandising
We are a family owned and operated wholesale company that has an "old fashioned" value - that serving the customer is the reason we are in business.
stw-wholesale.com/store.cfm

Regent Products
Regent Products Corp is a leader in the close-out and merchandising industry. Since 1985, we've been meeting our goal of providing retailers and wholesalers with consistent service and exceptional value.
www.regentproducts.com

Clothing

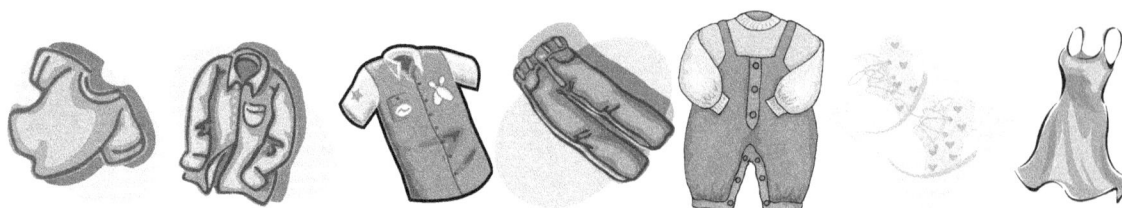

Aaron Maternity

Wholesale maternity clothes distributor in Albemarle, NC, USA. Includes Motherhood, Mimi and Pea in the Pod name brand maternity wear dresses, shorts, pants, jeans, tops, shirts, bathing suits, and sleepwear pregnancy clothes wholesale.

http://www.aaronmaternity.com

Adar Medical Uniforms

Wholesale American clothes supplier of medical uniforms based in Brooklyn, NYC, New York, USA. Supplies uniforms to the medical industry including lab coats, whites, medical scrubs, scrub sets, women's uniforms, men's uniforms, talls, solid tops, pants, skirts, men's labs, aprons, female uniform garments, twills, petites and other clothing for doctors, nurses, surgeons and other medical professionals.

http://www.adarmedicaluniforms.com

All Together Diapers

American baby diapers suppliers in Sandy, Utah 84070, USA. Includes a wide range of diapers and nappies including OsoCozy prefold, fitted, organic diapers, pins, snappies, pull on nappies, adult diapers and accessories for babies.

http://www.alltogetherdiaper.com

Clothing Continued

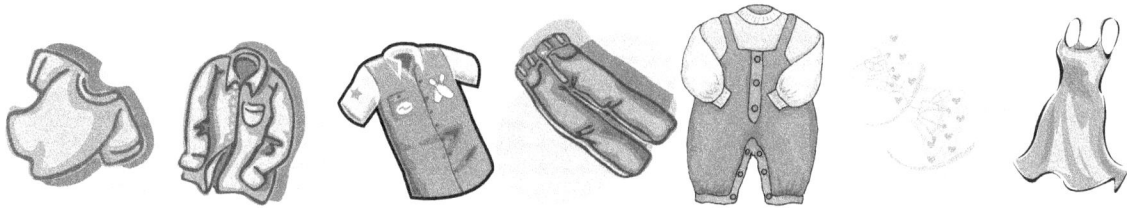

Anna's Preemie Clothes

American baby clothes suppliers in Colorado Springs, CO 80906-4050, USA. Specializing in preemie clothing, premature baby boys and girls bibs, dresses, suits, christening clothes, shirts, hats, bonnets, gowns, baby bag gowns, sleepers and other clothes for preemies or preterm babies.
http://www.annaspreemie.com

B & A Uniforms

Wholesale distributor of uniforms for work places that require medical, restaurant, casual, housekeeping, and industrial clothing.
http://www.bauniforms.com

Best Wholesale Lingerie

Wholesale American clothing supplier of undergarments and lingerie based in Valencia, CA 91355, USA. Products include plus size underwear, corsets, bustiers, big size sexy lingerie, bras, thongs, shape wear, hosiery, panties, baby dolls and sexy undergarments for women.
http://www.bestwholesalelingerie.com

Clothing Continued

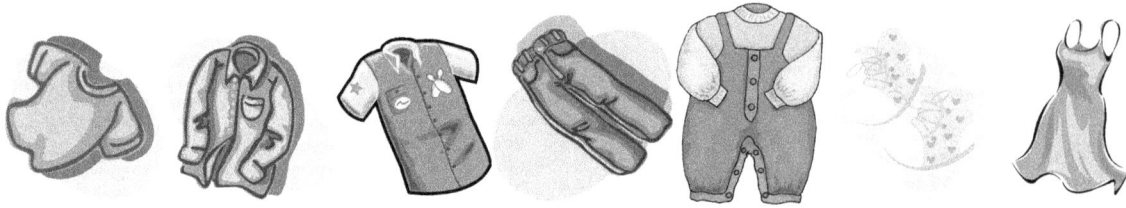

Chic Star

Sexy clothing wholesale from a USA based company. Includes a range of sexy fashion dresses, shirts, tops, sexy low rise pants, skirts, blazers and jackets for women, teens and girls.
http://www.chicstar.com

Children's Wholesale.com

Find wholesale children's clothing including formal wear, communion dresses, outerwear in a range of styles and colors, available online for purchase. American wholesaler located in Tampa, Florida.
http://www.childrenswholesale.com

C Mack Sports

US clothes suppliers of cheerleading uniforms located in Bloomsburg, Pa, USA. Supplies a range of stock cheer uniforms, motion wear uniforms, pompoms, warm ups, briefs, midriffs, cheer accessories, and custom team cheer outfits for schools and sporting teams.
http://www.cmacksports.com

Clothing Continued

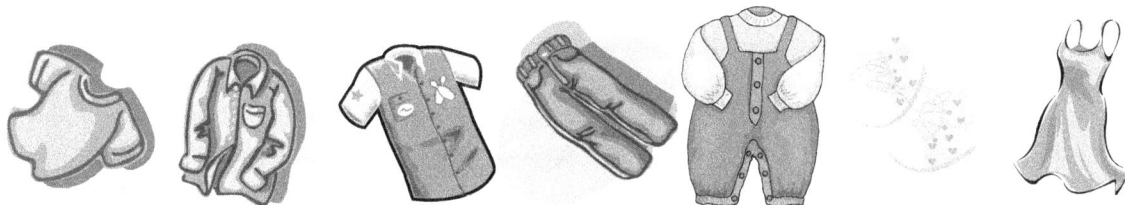

Crazy About Costumes

Costume wholesaler based in Saratoga Springs, Utah, USA. Offering masks, suits, and fancy dress suits for TV characters, superheroes, and holiday characters like Superman, Spider-man, Batman, Captain America, Harry Potter, Lord of the Rings, Fantastic 4, Sexy Costumes and more.

http://www.crazyaboutcostumes.com

Genuine School Uniforms

American clothing suppliers of wholesale school uniforms and accessories from the state of Florida. Supplies uniforms for students throughought the United States. School clothes for boys and girls includes dresses, skirts, school blazers, shirts, and clothing accessories for school kids.

http://www.genuineschooluniform.com

Hammars Uniform

Wholesale uniform company located in Troutdale, Oregon with screen printing and embroidery departments for hotel uniforms, restaurant uniforms, medical uniforms, and work uniforms.

http://www.hammarsuniform.com

Clothing Continued

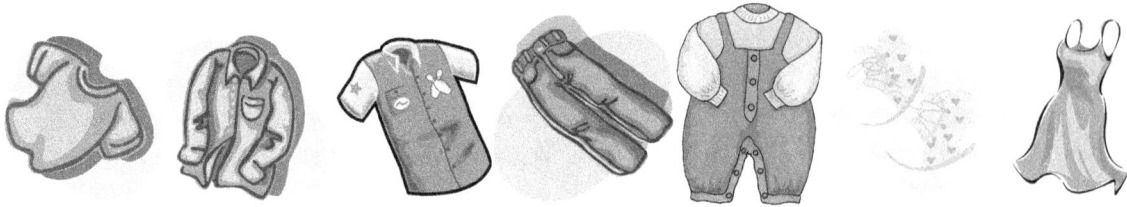

Hollywood Costumes

American wholesalers and retailers of Halloween costumes and disguises, theatre quality costumes, masks , wigs, hats, props, party supplies, Mardi Gras suits, factory direct in Florida.

http://www.hollywood-costumes.com

Jasmine USA Clothing

Plus size clothing wholesalers in Los Angeles, California, United States. Merchandise available includes women's plus size dresses, skirts, tops, and pants for big women and girls.

http://www.jasmineusaclothing.com

Clothing Continued

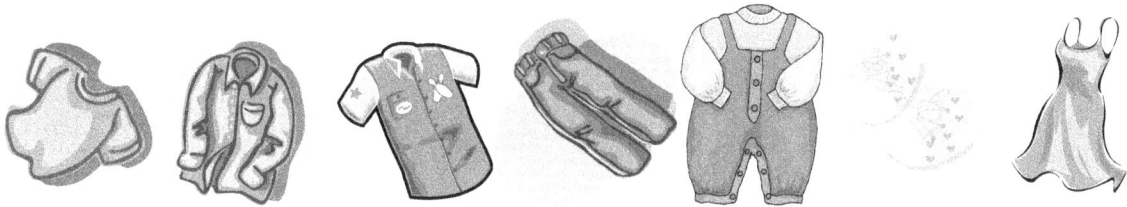

Jims Formal Wear

Wholesale formalwear rental company headquartered in Trenton, Illinois with tuxedo rentals for wedding, prom, black tie affair or other formal events.
http://www.jimsformalwear.com

Jones T- Shirts

Wholesale T -shirt company in Provo, Utah, USA. Selling wholesale T-shirts, tank tops, polos/golf shirts, ladies shirts, youth T-shirts and other blank, printable apparel.
http://www.jonestshirts.com

Kids Resource

Kids Resource is a children's wholesale clothing distributor of quality children's apparel in Largo, Florida, USA. Complete wholesaler source of children's wholesale clothing for retailers, worldwide, since 1985.
http://www.kidsresource.com

Clothing Continued

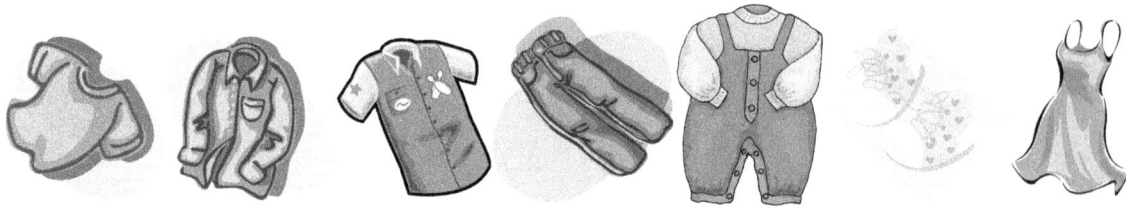

Kleids Enterprises, Inc.

Clothing manufacturer of American made women's wholesale clothing including organic clothing, travel wear, warm weather clothing, resort wear, beach wear, sportswear, ski resort wear, and casual clothing.
http://www.kleids.com

Mak Leathers

Wholesale coats and jackets from a company in Buffalo, New York. Includes bomber jackets, trench coats, leather jackets, and accessories to retailers.
http://www.makleather.com

My Leather

Leather jacket wholesalers in Los Angeles, California, United States. A large assortment of leather jackets, biker jackets, varsity and bomber jackets.
http://www.myleather.com

Clothing Continued

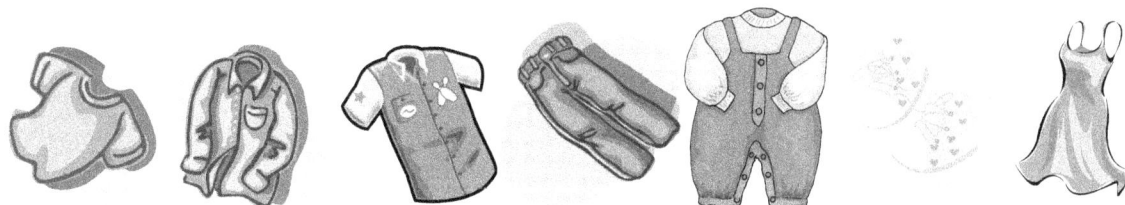

Nicole Maternity Wholesale

Florida based wholesaler of maternity clothing in the USA. Offers a range of clothes including maternity bridesmaid dresses, formal wear, swimwear, fashion for pregnant women, and maternity dresses.
http://www.nicolematernitywholesale.com

Penguin Kids Wear

American clothes wholesaler of children's apparel and off-price brand name kids clothing based in Los Angeles, CA, USA. Supplying pre-packed quantities to children clothing retailers. All products are first quality, brand new, and with tags.
http://www.wholesalechildrenclothing.com

Scrub n Prints

American medical uniforms wholesaler located in Delray Beach, FL, USA. Offers medical and nurse uniforms, scrubs apparel, scrub mate clothes, scrub lab coats, nurse aprons, gowns, and scrubs clothing for nurses, surgeons, and operating room personnel.
http://www.scrubnprints.com

Clothing Continued

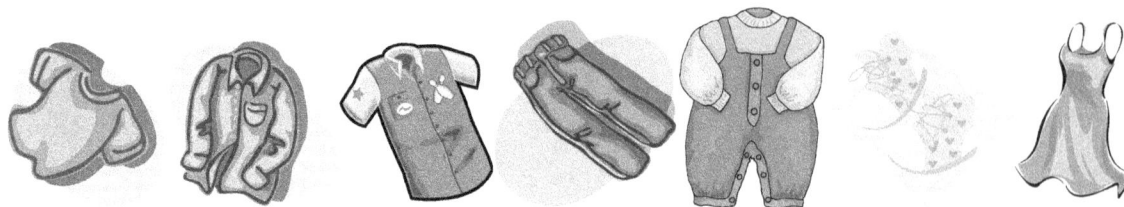

Sensual Mystique
Wholesale and drop shipping company based in California, USA. Offering a range of sexy lingerie, bridal lingerie, chemise, thongs, bras, corsets, garters, panties and more.
http://www.sensualmystique.com

Steal Deal
American wholesale urban clothing suppliers with offices in Los Angeles, California, USA. Supplies a large range of men's hip hop clothes, cheap urban wear, and industrial fashion from famous authentic clothes brands like Akademiks, Apple Bottoms, Enyce, Girbaud, Hot Air, Sean John and more. Products include hoodies, polos, long sleeve shirts, jeans, tshirts, pants, shoes and fashion accessories.
http://www.stealdeal.com

Swimsuit Station
USA wholesale clothes suppliers of plus size swimsuits and swimwear based in Ocean, New Jersey, USA. Supplying a range of big size swim wear, bikinis, board shorts, surf clothes, beach sarongs, cover ups and fashionable plus size swimsuits and bathing suits for women and men.
http://www.swimsuitstation.com

Clothing Continued

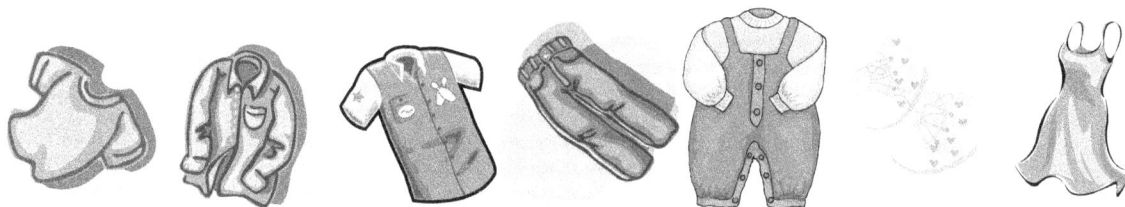

Sydney's Closet

American clothes company and wholesaler of plus size formal wear for women which includes prom dresses, homecoming outfits, weddings, dances, balls, holiday parties, and pageant clothing. Formal wear plus size clothing showroom located in St. Louis, Missouri.
http://www.sydneyscloset.com

TBIapparel.com

Featuring a wide selection of fashion and casual wholesale apparel and clothing for young men and women, plus size clothing, and more.
http://www.tbiapparel.com

Team Cheer

Wholesale cheerleading uniforms and accessories for cheerleaders located in NY USA. Find cheer shoes, cheerleading outfits, pom - poms, sports bags, and clothing accessories for girls, teens and women cheer leaders.
http://www.teamcheer.com

Clothing Continued

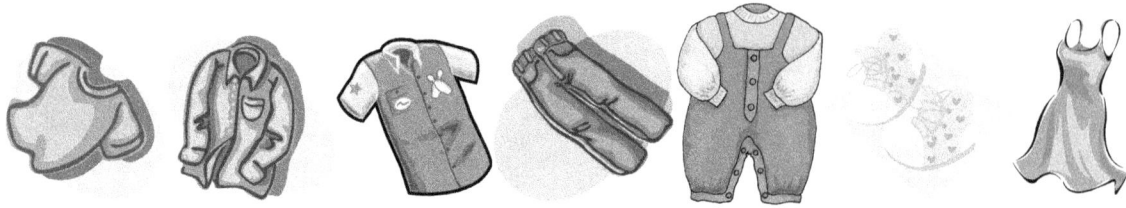

Tie Dye Temple

Wholesale tie dye clothing and accessories available from Westminster, Colorado, USA. Merchandise includes both retail and wholesale tie dyed t shirts, sarongs, American flags, bags, hats, panties, bed sheets, and tie dyed dresses for hippies and happy people.
http://www.tiedyetemple.com

Ujena Wholesale

Wholesale company with a range of swimwear in Mountain View, California. Includes a range of one piece swimmers, sexy bikinis, bathing suits, and cover ups for swimming and at the beach.
http://ujenawholesale.com

Western Express

US wholesale western clothing supply company based in Bridgeville, PA 15017 in the United States of America. Supplies a large range of American western style clothes and fashion, cowboy hats, country western accessories, cattleman hats, bolo ties, western belt buckles, bandanas, patriotic shirts, ponchos, American flags, leather wallets, leather purses, western shirts, t-shirts, sweaters, tank tops, suspenders, outerwear, leather vests, and other clothing made in the USA.
http://www.westernexpressinc.com

Clothing Continued

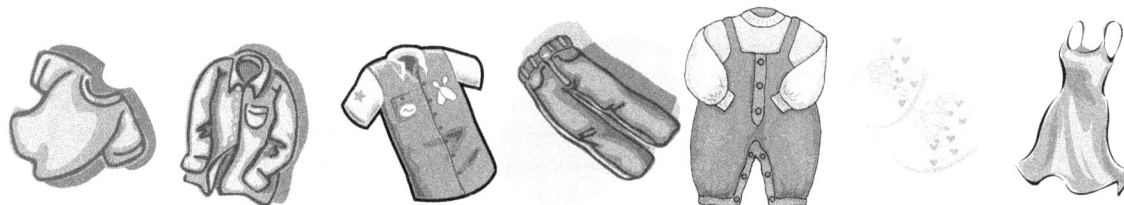

Whoa Mamma

USA wholesaler of maternity and nursing lingerie, loungewear and sleepwear. It was founded with the sole mission of giving new and expecting mothers the gift of feeling sexy and confident during a special time in their lives. Lingerie wholesalers based in Minnesota, USA.
http://www.whoamamma.com

Wholesale Baby Blanks

Manufacturer and wholesale distributor of blank infant garment for screen printing and embellishment. Wholesaler primarily distributes to USA and Canada with drop shipping available.
http://www.wholesalebabyblanks.com

Wholesale Clothing Market

US clothes wholesalers of urban and hiphop fashion based in the city of Miami, Florida, USA. Supplies a range of hoodies, tshirts, coats and jackets, jerseys, jeans, hats, caps, tops, polos, long sleeve shirts, shorts, pants, fashion accessories, and pullovers. Buy ladies and mens clothes and apparel from famous urban clothes clothing brands like Enyce, Pepe, Pelle Pelle, Girbaud, Sean John, Ecko, Akademiks, Phat Farm, Rocawear, Outkast, and more.
http://www.wholesaleclothingmarket.com

Clothing Continued

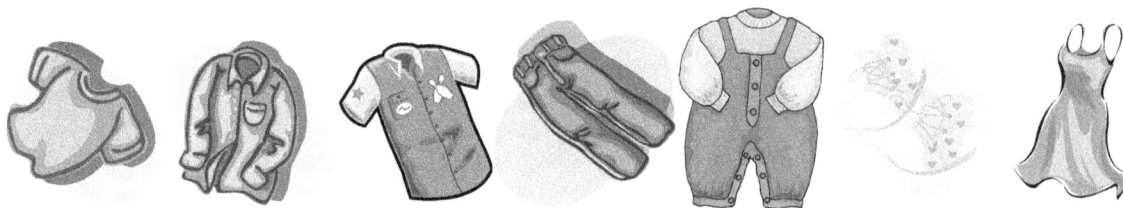

Wholesale Denim Jeans

Women's embellished and bejeweled jeans at wholesale from a Florida based company in America. Includes a range of empathy jeans and crystal jeans made from denim,in a variety of colors, patterns, and styles for women and girls.
http://www.wholesaledenimjeans.com

Wholesale Kid

American clothing wholesaler based in Kensington, Kansas, USA. Supplying newborn baby clothing, baby clothes, toddler merchandise, and children's clothing wholesale. Also a clothes drop shipper of kid's and children's clothing merchandise.
http://www.wholesalekid.com

Wyoming Traders

American wholesale clothes traders supplying western clothes and silk scarves, based in Afton, WY, USA. Wyoming traders stock silk scarf products, ties, western gear, rancher jackets, pommel slickers, barn jackets, coats, shirts, vests, denim jackets, rain slickers, parkas, wool caps, and outerwear.
http://www.wyomingtraders.com

Electronics

Cable Wholesale

American audio equipment suppliers in Livermore, CA 94551, USA. Specializing in cables, Cat 5 & Cat 6, HDMI, SVGA, DVI, USB, FireWire, security and fire alarm cables, speaker wire, bulk cable, microphone cables, microphones and more products, electronic components and accessories.
http://www.cablewholesale.com

Mega Goods

American wholesale company and electronics dropshippers based in Los Angeles, CA, USA supplying a large range of electronics. Products include Apple iPods, iPod accessories, portable TVs, cellular phones, car audio, DVD players, televisions, RC cars, digital cameras, game consoles like the Nintendo Wii, Xbox 360, and Sony Play Station.
http://www.megagoods.com

Scan Sound

Distributor of electrical supplies in Deerfield Beach, FL 33442, USA. Specializing in headphones, ipod headphones, stereo ear phone, ear pads, ear buds, mono, single ear stereo earphones, rubber ear tips, mri earphones, acoustic foam ear tips and related audio accessories.
http://www.scansound.com

Electronics Continued

West Virginia Electric Supply Company
Distributor of electrical supplies in the USA in Huntington, West Virginia is a Cooper master distributor for fusing and arresters in the electronics industry. Merchandise available include arresters, cutouts, NX fuses, insulators, contacts parts, NX capacitor fuse, fuse-ARC stranglers, mountings, RTE expulsion bayonet fuse links, and more.
http://wvesco.com

Petra Industries
Your 'one stop' accessory source for consumer electronics and accessories, including car audio and satellite product. We also carry appliance connection parts and hookup supplies.
www.petra.com

Simba Electronics
We are a wholesale only distributor of electronics. If you are a retailer, we urge you to visit or call us today.
www.simbaelectronics.com

Electronics Continued

Ramko Distributors
Full service National Consumer Electronics Distributor specializing in car stereo , CB radios, radar detectors, scanners, 10 meter radios, antennas, mobile videos, and more. Dealers and wholesale only.
www.ramkodist.com

Capitol Sales
National hybrid supplier for over 100 manufacturers in consumer electronics, custom home theatre, telecommunications and home automation.
www.capitolsales.com

Thunderball Marketing
Wholesale Electronics, Camcorders, Stereos, TV, Car Stereos, DJ, Audio, Auto Alarms, Auto Security, Auto Stereo, Speakers, Home Stereo, Radio, Cellular, Phones, Mixers, Auto Speakers, Auto Amplifiers, Auto Equalizers.
www.tball.com

Electronics Continued

CB Distributing
CB Distributing is a wholesale distributor of wireless communications and other electronics.
www.cbdistributing.com

Dragon Distributing
Dragon Distributing distributors of radar detectors, telephones, car audio, car audio accessories, CB radios, CB accessories, scanners, televisions, games, inverters, 12 volt travel, batteries, audio.
www.dragondistributing.com

H.L. Dalis
H.L. Dalis is the nation's oldest multi-line wholesale distributor of consumer electronics, industrial electronics and related products.
www.hldalis.com

Electronics Continued

MCM

MCM an InOne company is a leading distributor of electronic components, surplus and value-added services.
mcm.newark.com

Consumer Electronic Distributors

Wholesale electronics distributor, largest JVC distributor for the Midwest.
www.cedincorp.com

Electronics Continued

Tri State Distributors
Tri State Distributors provides wholesale consumer electronics from many fine manufacturers.
www.tristatedistributors.com/products/electronics.html

Electronics Distributors
Quality, brand-name equipment and factory direct pricing. Same-day shipments, no minimums.
www.e-d-c.com

Koby International
Koby International Inc. opens doors to new technologies. Order the best car stereo, car audio products you need at the best wholesale prices to satisfy your customers.
www.koby-international.com

Electronics Continued

Bursma Electronics
For over 50 years, Bursma Electronics has been a proud supplier of audio/video components and accessories to thousands of customers across the United States.
www.bursma.com

Buy 4 Less Electronics
Buy 4 Less Electronics is a wholesale distributor of name-brand Consumer Electronics, Photo, and Computer products.
www.buy4lessinc.com

Electronics Continued

Fashion Electronics

Importer and wholesaler of small electronics and premium gifts.
www.fashionelectronics.com

Horne Co

Ron Horne Company - electronics distributor.
www.ronhorne.com

CWR Electronics

CWR Electronics is a wholesale electronics distributor, a specialty electronics distributor and consumer electronics distributors of wholesale electronics.
www.cwrelectronics.com

Electronics Continued

Volutone Distributing
Consumer electronics and supplies for the home, business and auto in the western United States.
www.volutone.com

TeleDynamics LLP
Telephone Wholesale Distributor for Panasonic Business Telephone Systems, Siemens gigaset cordless phones, Sony consumer electronics, AT&T telecommunication equipment, Vtech and Uniden 900MHz.
www.teledynamics.com

JNL Trading Inc.
We are a consumer electronics wholesaler. We carry brand named items such Panasonic, Minolta, Olympus, Fuji, Canon, Samsung, Lexmark and many more.
www.jnlelectronic.com

Electronics Continued

Alltronics

Alltronics was founded in July 1978 and is in the business of selling and buying electronic components and equipment. A large portion of our business is mail order and wholesale to other dealers worldwide.
www.alltronics.com

Gamla Enterprises

North Americas premier dealer / distributor of photographic and electronic equipment since 1989, with over 15,000 satisfied retailers.
www.gamlaphoto.com

eBuyRite.com

Your Direct source for all MultiSystem -220V products. Over 20 years in business.
www.ebuyrite.com

Electronics Continued

DAABS Electronics Inc.
We are the established leader of wholesale electronics distribution in the multi-system 110/220 volt market for over 20 years, for the United States and overseas.
www.daabsusa.com

DigiGear, Inc.
We are your one stop source for all of your digital and lenticular products (3D Photo Print; EZ3D Photo Print). We stock all digital camera accessories, including flash card adapters and readers.
www.digigearinc.com

Perfumes & Fragrance

For centuries people have been intrigued by various fragrances. Fragrances and perfumes are always popular selling products that are often advertised as the key to success in life, love and work. "Imposter" fragrances have gained in popularity and also in similarity to the name brand for a fraction of the cost. Certain fragrances are known to stir memories of childhood, holidays, love, romance and more. Selling fragrances and perfumes may attract a steady flow of customers as well as repeat business and referrals.

Perfume Center of America
The Perfume Center of America carries a huge inventory of about 1600 brand-name perfume and colognes.
www.perfume-center.com

Designer Fragrances
We are one of the largest distributors of fragrances and colognes and have one of the world largest selections in the USA.
www.designerfragrancesinc.com

French Look International
French Look International Inc. is an importer and exclusive wholesale distributor of fragrance and personal care product lines from Europe.
www.frenchlook.com

Paris Fragrance
Paris Fragrance is an international wholesaler. We offer a wide selection of name brand Fragrances, Perfumes, Colognes , After Shave, Body Lotions, Body Powder, Bath & Shower Gel, Bath Oil, Massage Oil, Cosmetics and Makeup Sets.
www.pfragrance.com

Perfumes & Fragrance Continued

FragranceNet.com
Your source for discount perfumes, discount colognes, designer fragrances, pheromone colognes and designer perfumes.
www.fragrancenet.com

Eddie's Perfume & Cosmetic
Eddies Perfume is a distributor of brand name fragrances for men and women. We supply hundreds of businesses around the world with quality, designer merchandise at very competitive prices.
www.eddiesperfume.peachhost.com/home.htm

Jane Bernard Aromatics
Jane Bernard Aromatics is your place for "scentsational" gifts and other delights. We have been among the leaders in quality home fragrance products.
www.janebernardwholesale.com

Perfumes & Fragrance Continued

Paradise Fragrances Mfg.
Wholesale perfume oils, body fragrances, perfume body oils all below wholesale.
www.paradisefragrances.com

The House of Fragrances
Distributors, manufacturers, and wholesalers of fragrance oils for the body, fragrance oils for candle and soap-making, incense, fragranced lotions, shower gels, bath crystals, and personal care products.
www.thehouseoffragrances.com

Perfumes & Fragrance Continued

Fragrance Wholesale

Since 1986, we have been a leading wholesaler/retailer of designer fragrances and cosmetics. This presence in the wholesale marketplace has enabled us to sell both directly and indirectly to large chain retailers.
www.fragrancewholesale.com

Luxury Perfumes Wholesale

22+ years Wholesale/Retail experience - 60 store locations worldwide. Over 10,000 Designer Wholesale fragrances, Hard to find, Gift sets. 100% Authentic, Worldwide/International Shipping, 24 hour orders. Trust our name and service at Luxury Perfumes. Watch our video on the about us page. 877 SCENT LA (723 6852)
www.luxuryperfume.com

Atlantic Perfumes Wholesale

Atlantic Perfumes Wholesale is a leading wholesale distributor of brand name perfumes, colognes, fragrance gift sets, testers and bath & body products. We have over 10 years of experience in the wholesale perfume industry.
www.perfumes-wholesale.com

Gift Baskets

QCU One Stop Wholesale
Wholesale baskets and gift supply, gourmet food basket supply and gift basket supply are available from QCU.
www.qcustore.com

Gift Basket Supplies Inc1
We are the inventors and original manufacturers of the fitted basketbag. Buy direct from the manufacturer.
www.gift-basket-supplies.com

Country Baskets Imports
Country Baskets Imports is an importer, wholesaler and manufacturer of beautiful hand-woven baskets.
www.basketsimports.com

Pioneer Wholesale Co
Pioneer Wholesale Co specializes in silks, baskets, containers, and ribbon. We stock some 3000 items from new to unique to utilitarian.
www.pioneerwholesaleco.com

Giftware

Giftware offers a great assortment of merchandise or you may decide to specialize in just one area such as globes or picture frames.

There also are numerous giftware tradeshows throughout the US where you can meet the vendors and see their wares firsthand.

Mitech Trading
We are distributors and wholesalers of promotional products and gifts.
www.mitechtrading.com

Napa Valley Wholesale
Napa Valley Wholesale has been providing quality gift items since 1997. We specialize in fine gifts including custom and personalized items.
www.napavalleywholesale.com

Naleka Gifts
Since 1990, Naleka Pewter ware & Gifts has served our satisfied customers with the highest quality handcrafted pewter ware at wholesale prices.
www.pewterwholesale.com

Stop n Browse
We are a wholesale novelty and gifts supplier to the resale trade. Our customers include retailers, distributors, flea market and swap meet vendors, as well as individuals wanting to start their own novelty and gift business.
www.stopnbrowse.com

Giftware Continued

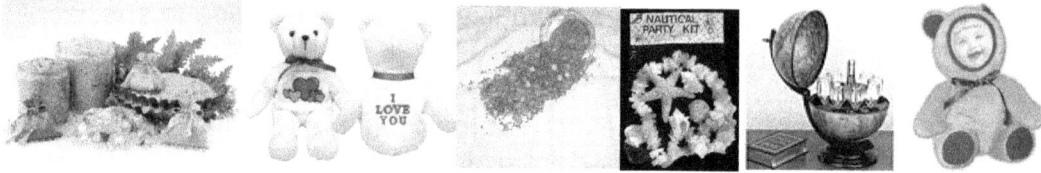

LTD Commodities

LTD Commodities LLC shops the world to bring you the best merchandise at tremendous value prices. And when you order in lots of three or more, you save on shipping.
www.ltdcommodities.com

Adams Wholesale

Our goal is to supply high quality gift, collectible and home decor products at low prices. We strive to keep YOUR business on the cutting edge!
www.adamswholesale.com

G&Z International

We are importers and wholesalers of gift items and artificial flowers.
www.gzintlinc.com

BuyGDI.com

Offers a large selection of unique gifts, home & garden decor, porcelain dolls, dragon figurines, vases, bookends, birdhouses and feeders, curios, mirrors, angel collectibles, religious gifts and more special occasion gifts at discount and wholesale prices.
www.buygdi.com

Shell Horizons Inc.

US Largest Wholesaler of Seashells and Ocean Products.
www.shellhorizons.com

Giftware Continued

Affordable Art and Crafts
Provider of wholesale giftware for retail gift shops, travel plazas, zoos, aquariums, pharmacies and individual purchasers.
www.affordablegiftware.com

Khan Imports
Khan Imports has provided the wholesale gift and decorative accessory industry with beautifully handcrafted, unique gifts, natural stone sculptures, marble chess sets, wildlife and animal collectible's and high quality home decor since 1989.
www.khanimports.com/wholesale.html

Couronne Company
Wholesale glass manufacturer distributor offering extensive line of glassware.
www.glassnow.com

Howard Wholesale
New wholesale items just released. Gifts, collectibles, candles, musicals, angels, dolls, toys, solid 14K Jewelry, much more. Updated Monthly. Always a discount and a free gift on every order.
howpro.safeshopper.com

Ohio Wholesale
Your source of wholesale giftware, country crafts and other gifts. We have everything from wholesale baskets and wall pockets to primitive country items, wholesale wreaths and much more wholesale giftware items.
www.ohiowholesale.com

Giftware Continued

Star International
Specializes in hand painted giftware with a strong focus on aquarium, nautical and tropical designs.
www.star91.com

Asian World Imports
Asian World Imports seeks to bring you the finest crafts from the ethnic tribal groups and artisans of India, Nepal, Thailand and Vietnam.
www.asianworldimports.com

Blue Seas Trading
Seashells and much more available on a wholesale basis to souvenir and gift shops as well as sea shell collectors.
www.blueseasonline.com

Handvision
Importer of fiber optics, novelty lighting and home decorations.
www.handvision.com

Siskiyou Gifts
Specializing in the finest cast pewter products available. From belt buckles to glassware, from jewelry to licensed sports products.
www.siskiyougifts.com

Giftware Continued

Wholesale Gifts

We are leading direct importer, exporter, wholesaler of jewelry, gifts, unique giftware, Bali arts and crafts, home decorating, garden accessory, musical instrument, handmade giftware products, jewelry and fashion accessories, sarong and beachwear, Indonesia tribal art.
www.wholesalejewelryfinding.com

VIP Wholesale

Sells unique gifts that include lifelike furry animals made out of rabbit or sheep pelt, feather products, crystal gifts, book ends.
www.vipwholesale.com

Crystal Florida

Crystal Florida is a leading manufacturer and importer of crystal gift items, committed to maintaining high standards and quality for which we have been known since 1951.
www.crystalflorida.com

Levine Gifts

Levine Gifts wholesales tart burners, potpourri burners, tart warmers, electric tart burners, electric tart warmers, candle warmers, wax potpourri tarts, jar & votive candle accessories.
www.levinegifts.com

Union Trading Co

We offer a unique line of fine handcrafted needlepoint and beaded products to gift retailers around the world.
www.uniontrading.com

Giftware Continued

Premier Gift Ltd

Premier Gift Ltd is a wholesale giftware distributor that sells only to retail stores in Canada and the United States. Stores may request catalogues and pricing information.
www.premier-gift.com

Bank Makers

Manufacturer of realistic animal piggy banks and dog and cat ornaments.
www.bankmakers.com

Water and Wood

Water and Wood Inc. is a direct importer, distributor and wholesaler of giftware items for the wholesale industry. We offer unique high quality gifts at great prices.
www.waterandwood.com

plazaQ.com

plazaQ.com is designed for origami, Chinese medicine or gift resellers who would like to purchase items directly from the Internet.
www.plazaq.com

World Glass Imports

Large selection of glass sculptures.
www.worldglassimports.com

Giftware Continued

KC Company Ltd

The premier wholesale distributor for Hawaiian gifts and souvenirs. Our site now offers you both retail and wholesale services.
www.kchawaii.com

Chico Arts

Specializes in Mandalas, dream catchers, key chains, velvet paintings, leather paintings, shields, porcelain dolls, painted pots, blankets, ponchos, Mexican fables, rugs.
www.chicoarts.com

The Music Box Shop

The Music Box Shop - wholesale music boxes to buyers of quantity.
www.musicboxeswholesale.com

World One - USA

Featuring Cooper craft Pottery of Stoke-on-Trent, England. Cooper craft is known as specialist manufacturer of hand crafted English bone china products.
www.worldone.us

Flowers Inc. Balloons

Flowers Inc. Balloons - The world's largest wholesale balloon and coordinating gift supplier.
www.flowersincballoons.com

Giftware Continued

Legend Dairy Clothing Store & Wholesaler

Drop shipper new born baby gift line. Official Licensee of Got Milk? One piece lap shoulder, bibs, burp towels, baby caps, Hospital Promotional Gifts. Toxic Free replacement nipples, pacifiers, multi-stage feeders. Baby safe glass bottles. Youth, teens, adults. V-neck t, tank tops, t shirts, low cut spaghetti strap t, Sweat Shirts. Coffee mugs, milk glasses, laminated photo clocks and more.
www.legenddairy.net

Incense

Used for centuries, incense continues to be a popular seller. There are many different scents and also accessories. There are also Native American products such as white sage and other herbs used as smudge sticks that are quite popular. It is wise to educate yourself on the different types and different qualities available. Some people buy the ingredients and make their own incense. Some scents are more popular than others and the accessories such as incense burners also make great gifts. Incense can be a repeat business for many resellers.

Miracle Incense Co
Our Purpose as an incense wholesaler is to provide your company with high quality products, strong customer support, and competitive wholesaler prices.
www.miracleincense.com

GFD Imports
Wild Berry Incense Distributor - The best online shopping source for incense and accessories.
www.incensewholesale.com

Matt's Incense
The largest manufacturer and supplier of incense and related products. Massive inventory and amazing wholesale prices.
www.mattsincense.com

River Village
We are wholesalers of incense, incense burners, tapestries, flags, and other novelties at a great price. Get a free catalog.
www.river-village.com/wholesale.html

Incense Continued

Sweet Rock
For over 30 years, Sweet Rock® scented products have been a perfect match for the flea market, swap meet, and specialty market vendors.
www.sweetrock.com

Scents Of Paradise
We are one of the largest manufacturers of alcohol free incense in the USA. We carry a large selection of wood punk, charcoal and colored incense sticks and cones in a variety of sizes.
www.scentsofparadise.com

Smokey Mountain Incense
Our company is 3 years old manufacturing an older established line of powdered incense and burners. We use only quality uncut fragrance oils for maximum fragrance delivery.
www.smtn.us

Laxmi Incense
Laxmi Incense has been a leading importer and wholesale supplier of the finest incense in the world for more than 30 years. We are famous for carrying superior quality incense products.
www.laxmiincense.com

Military Surplus

Mad Dog Wholesale

Mad Dog Wholesale is the wholesale provider of military, federal, state and local government liquidated surplus. Our inventory changes weekly and includes clothing, equipment, and fire/law enforcement gear.
www.maddogonline.com

MSH

Military Supply House.com has one of the largest selections of military surplus in the United States. over 3 million items in stock. We ship almost anywhere.
www.militarysupplyhouse.com

Knife Vault Wholesale

Large selection of knives at wholesale.

www.knifevaultwholesale.com

Rothco

Huge selection of military and camo.

Over 4,000 items in their dealer wholesale catalog

www.rothco.com/wholesale

Toy & Novelty Items

Toys are always popular sellers especially around the holidays. If you are able to stock the hottest most popular toys you may attract more customers. Special promotions can be created to entice people to buy more such as quantity discounts.

One Stop Toy Co
We are a direct importer of toys as well as one of the largest distributors of candy on the west coast.
www.toysandcandy.com

Toy Wonders Inc.
Toy Wonders Inc. is a manufacturer, an importer and a distributor of toys, novelties, and select gifts to wholesale distributors and retail stores.
www.toywonders.net

Esco Imports Inc.
Esco Imports is an importer and distributor of wholesale toys and novelties.
www.escoimports.com

American Chess Store
American Chess Store offers chess sets, chess books, chess clocks, chess pieces, & computers as well as backgammon, cribbage and casino equipment.
www.americanchessstore.com

Toys & Novelty Items Continued

Safari Ltd
Safari Ltd is the premier wholesaler of dinosaur and animal replicas, science toys and other educational and creative products.
www.safariltd.com

Play Visions
Play Visions Inc. - Importer and Distributor of Toys and Novelties.
www.playvisions.us

Toy Depot
We have been a major Los Angeles wholesaler and distributor of toys for over 20 years. Our toys are factory direct so that our customers don't have to look further for the best value.
store.toydepotinc.com

Playtime CWE
Playtime CWE has been in business for eight years selling high quality plush animals.
www.wholesaleplush.com

Toys & Novelty Items Continued

Mary Meyer Toys
Clever and collectible stuffed bears and toys from Mary Meyer.
www.marymeyer.com

Fiesta Toy
Fiesta Toy Company, stuffed animals, wholesale distributors and toy manufacturer.
www.fiestatoy.com

Fame Products
We are your supplier of quality traditional games such as dominoes, mahjongg, chess, backgammon, cribbage, and casino games.
www.fameproducts.com

Toy Smith
Toy Smith features a 274 page catalog filled with full-color photos of the over 1,400 items featured in the Toy Smith line.
www.toysmith.com

Toys & Novelty Items Continued

Best Buy George
Refrigerator magnets. World's largest manufacturer. Thousands of images.
www.bestbuygeorge.com

Ms. Teddy Bear
Manufacturer and wholesaler of stuffed animals. 13 years of experience, we specialize in fine quality teddy bears and stuffed animals for all events. Bear sizes range from 4" to 50" as low as $0.50 ea.
www.teddybearwholesale.com

American Folk Toys
American Folk Toys, Games, Crafts & Music is a historically based company dedicated to the preservation, nurture and development of traditional American folk toys.
www.amfolktoys.com

Dasaq Inc.
Wholesale brand name toys. Toy collectibles, action figures, dolls, plush, anime, backpacks. Wholesale toys for children and kids of all ages at below wholesale and closeout prices.
www.dasaq.com

Toys & Novelty Items Continued

Arrowcopter Inc.
Made in the United States, the original Arrowcopter Toy is attractively packaged in clear bubble pack, easy to display, easy to find.
www.arrowcopter.com

Binkley Toys
Get your ideas manufactured into a custom stuffed toy by one of the leading plush toy manufacturers, Custom Plush Toys.com.
www.customplushtoys.com

Bulk Toy Store
Discount toys, novelties, plush teddy bears, stickers, tattoos and more.
www.bulktoystore.com

Copernicus Toys
Unusual toys, gifts, puzzles and novelties for the inquisitive mind.
www.copernicustoys.com

Toys & Novelty Items Continued

Toys-n-Things
Fine wood toys including throw tops, Fiddlestixs connector toys, Gearworks gear construction toys, Amaze-n-marbles run toys, Frontier log cabin building sets, Kinder logs and blocks, and Teepees.
www.toys-n-things.com

Plush in Rush
Plush in a Rush is wholesale plush toy and animal distributor and importer specializing in plush animals, wholesale valentine products, homecoming mum supplies, and plush high school mascots.
www.plushinarush.com

Master Toys and Novelties
Master Toys and Novelties Inc. is located in Los Angeles and has been a manufacturer, direct importer, and wholesaler of toys, dolls, novelty gift items, and die-cast metal cars for over 30 years.
www.mastertoysinc.com

John Hansen Company
We have been providing best-selling toys and games to the market for more than 50 years. Our experience enables us to bring our customers leading brands at the best possible value.
www.johnhansenco.com

Toys & Novelty Items Continued

Sunny Toy & Gift
Sunny Toy & Gift is a toy manufacturer, direct importer as well as distributor. We are specialized in but not limited to plush and stuffed toys.
www.sunnytoyandgift.com

Peek-A-Boo Toys
Peek-A-Boo Toys, Ltd. designs, develops, markets, and distributes plush toys and pillows.
www.peekabootoys.com

Boley Corporation
Boley incorporated in California in the year 1981. We manufacture, import and distribute various kinds of high quality toys and novelties.
www.boleycorp.com

Toys & Novelty Items Continued

Warehouse 36
WAREHOUSE 36 has teamed up with select manufacturers to provide you with the ultimate dealer experience. Great products, great service and great people.
www.warehouse36.com

Tara Toy Corp
Tara Toy Corporation is a manufacturer of toys and party favors. We were founded in 1977.
www.taratoy.com

O.K. Toys
O.K. Toys Inc. is a manufacturer, importer, exporter and a distributor of toys, novelties, and die-cast metal replicas.
www.oktoys.com

Toys & Novelty Items Continued

RMK Sales
Now in our 19th year, we are known worldwide for having unique merchandise at a highly competitive price point.
www.rmksales.com

Emily Toys
No description available.
www.emilytoysinc.com

Galaxy Distributors
Huge selection of toys. Ranging from cars to wristbands and everything in between. Top quality toys.
www.galaxytoys.com

Bruder Toys America
Bruder Toys is one of the largest family owned and operated manufacturers of high quality toys. Bruder Toys continues its commitment to remain one of the most reliable, specialty toy manufacturers in the world.
www.brudertoysamerica.com

Toys & Novelty Items Continued

Manley Toy Direct
Great toys for all ages at affordable wholesale prices.
www.manleytoy.com

Lotto Fun
We sell only the Hottest Novelties and General Merchandise in the USA and around the World.
www.noveltieswholesale.com

Accoutrements
For over 20 years, we've been providing our customers with an exciting selection of exclusive items and a friendly brand of customer service that prides itself on fast and accurate order fulfillment.
www.accoutrements.com

Novelty Poster
Your only source for posters, animated toys, gifts, novelties, singing hamsters, dancing hamsters.
www.noveltyposter.com

Toys & Novelty Items Continued

Jan Reed Sales

We have the number one selling stuffed plush animated singing musical frog. Frog to dog, horse to hare, pig to bear stuffed animals will work wonders to increase your sales.
www.2funstuff.com

UJ Trading Wholesale

Offering a variety of specialty retail and wholesale items, UJ Trading specializes in the latest, greatest and hottest import toys.
www.ujtrading.com

US Toy Co

Sells a vast array of carnival/party and seasonal decorations, novelty toys, stuffed animals, balloons and many more items that have been developed by us for our exclusive sale.
www.ustoy.com

Toys Wholesale.net

Import and Wholesale of quality Educational Toys, Puzzles, wooden toys, jigsaw puzzle, children toys, children games, kids' preschool learning toys.
www.toyswholesale.net

Toys & Novelty Items Continued

Hayes Specialties
We offer the best in Novelties and Toys not to mention commercial food service equipment.
www.ehayes.com

Long Island Novelties
Long Island Novelties is a Wholesale, Manufacturer, Importer and Exporter of Novelty items.
www.longislandnovelties.com

LeRoux Products
LeRoux Products - Carnival, toys and novelties.
www.lerouxproducts.com

Indeglow
Source for all your glow and novelty products.
www.indeglow.com

Toys & Novelty Items Continued

3Eagles Trading
Your source for Native American promotional items and crafts.
www.3eagles.org

Easton Enterprises
We are one of the largest glow product distributors in the country.
www.glowrus.com

R & S Industries
Miracle Polishing Cloth, 504% profits. Sell direct, chains, crews, kiosks, mail order, and fundraising.
www.miraclepolishingcloth.com

Cool Things Corp
We are the worldwide provider of today's hottest new novelties and gifts.
www.coolites.com

Toys & Novelty Items Continued

BobbleFactory.com
Custom bobble heads factory direct. Design your own bobblehead.
www.bobblefactory.com

Cavalieri Distributors
Cavalieri Distributors is a wholesale distributor selling to convenience/drug stores and stationary stores for over 13 yrs.
www.cavalieridistributors.com

Blacklight.com
We offer novelty lighting, figurines, chess sets, incense burners, digital scales, rolling papers, blunt wraps, black lights, posters, novelty ashtrays, Zippos, and other items.
www.blacklight.com

Panaria.com
Panaria, direct importers and THE ULTIMATE SOURCE for the NEWEST and the HOTTEST novelty, toy & gift items.
www.panaria.com

Toys & Novelty Items Continued

U-NEAK Inc.
U-neak.com sells signs, flags, windsocks and other novelties and gifts.
www.u-neak.com

Rebecca's
Rebecca's is a novelty wholesaler providing discount prices on novelties, toys, glow products, custom imprinting, puzzles & games, carnival supplies, jewelry, jokes, inflatables and gifts.
www.rebeccas.com

Akron Novelty
Akron Novelty & Merchandise Co has been serving our customers for the past 50 years as a novelty wholesale distributor and wholesale novelty item supplier.
www.akron-novelty.com

Mills Trading
Wholesale importer and novelty distributor. Your source for wholesale products.
www.millstrading.com

Toys & Novelty Items Continued

Novelty Specialists
We are dedicated to providing top quality products and unmatched service. Our long reaching broker network is always available to answer your every need.
www.noveltyspecialists.com

Sure Glow
Sure Glow is a wholesale distributor of glow in the dark products including: glow sticks, glow necklaces, magnetic light products, flashing body lights, light sticks, glow sticks, glow bracelets, strobes, glow in the dark party product supplies, light sticks, and other glow in the dark novelty items.
www.sureglow.com

Marco Novelty
Wholesale distributors of toys, jewelry, perfume, purses, costume jewelry, novelties, gifts, figurines, sterling silver, watches, flags, dollar store merchandise, closeouts, vintage items, collectibles.
planttel.net/~boyce/index.html

Lakeside Products
Lakeside Products is an importer, manufacturer and wholesaler of gifts, novelties and housewares.
www.lakesidenovelty.com

Toys & Novelty Items Continued

Meier & Frank Merchandise
A wholesale souvenir company, importers of flags, cloisonné pins, hat tacs and pencil sharpeners. Producers of souvenir items for all 50 US States.
www.meierfrank.com

Cruising International
Manufacturer, Wholesaler, Exporter of Souvenirs, Gifts, Novelties, and Collectables.
www.cruising-intl.com

Fun Friends
Fun Friends offers the hottest cell phone accessories, cell phone covers, plush characters, perfect novelty item and a unique gift idea for people of all ages.
www.funfriends.com

Mad Al Distributors
Mad Al Distributors is a wholesaler of Gundam Models, both Gundam and Gundam Wing, by Bandai.
www.madal.com

Toys & Novelty Items Continued

Rhode Island Novelty
Rhode Island Novelty is the nation's leading direct importer and wholesale distributor of novelties and toys.
www.rinovelty.com

Novelty Liquidators
Novelty Liquidators - Providing Value Priced Closeouts & Wholesale Novelties For Every Occasion.
www.noveltyliquidators.com

Franco American Novelty
Browse our site and view our current line of fine Costumes and Accessories with the launch of our two new costume collections.
www.francoamericannovelty.com

Perry Blackburne Inc.
Keychain wholesaler and importer of key accessories, key rings, split rings, carabineers, magnetic key cases, snap key rings and wrist coils.
www.perryblackburne.com

Toys & Novelty Items Continued

Dry Gulch

We have been producing quality novelty gifts for 20 years. Located in the Ozark Mountains we strive to let the ingenuity, craftsmanship and humor of our mountain heritage come through with the novelties we sell.
www.drygulchgifts.com

Escapade International

We are your wholesale source for novelties, die cast items, toys and lots more! Providing the latest and most popular products at the lowest wholesale prices resulting in incredible profits.
www.escapadeintl.com

Flashmans Inc.

Your one stop e-shop for everything that lights up or glows.
www.flashmanslights.com

Gadget Wholesalers

We are Wholesalers of The Doze Alert, a Sleep Warning Device for Motorists, Calorie and Heart Rate Watch, FN Radio Digital Sports Watch and Electronic Voice Recording Tape Measure. We Drop ship.
www.gadgetwholesalers.com

Toys & Novelty Items Continued

Light Up Shop
From Glow Products to Light up Jewelry and hundreds of other products we're your one-stop shop via the Internet. We have an exclusive relationship with nation's leading importer and wholesale distributor of novelty toys.
www.lightupshop.com

Arts & Crafts

Candles and Supplies

American soap making and candle making supplies company based in Quakertown, Pennsylvania, USA. Suppliers of a range of candle making products, wax, candle jars, wicks, colors, candle molds, and gel, along with soap making supplies like soap molds, starter kits, soap bases, liquid soap, oils, butters, additives, and other soap making accessories.
www.candlesandsupplies.net

Craft Hobby Wholesale

Large American arts and crafts wholesaler in Carson, CA., 90745 USA. Supplies a wide range of craft supplies, office supplies, back to school products, scrapbooking materials, scrapbook paper, patterns, glue sticks, sewing supplies, buttons, pens, closeouts, stickers, paint brushes, beads, beading supplies, art and craft start kits, scissors, art paint sets, pencils, and other materials and craft products.
www.crafthobbywholesale.com

D&L Art Glass Supply

US suppliers of art glass materials and supplies in Denver, Colorado, USA. Provides a range of glassmaking supplies, stained glass products, closeout supplies, kiln forming products, lampworking, irons, solders, chemicals, mosaic kits, glass breakers, cutters, and glass tools and equipment.
www.dlstainedglass.com

Arts & Crafts Continued

Pueblo Direct

Wholesale native American jewelry and ethnic gift products from a company based in Rio Rancho, New Mexico 87124, USA. Supplies a range of Native American jewelry like earrings, beads, necklaces, pendants, Southwest jewelry, bolo ties, belt buckles, watches, Zuni jewelry, and other Indian jewelry. Also supplies ethnic gifts, pottery products, Pueblo pottery, Hopi pottery, Zuni, Navajo, Santa Domingo, horse hair pottery, and other vases and pots. Along with Kachinas, fetishes, Kachina dolls, sand art, and Native American Indian artifacts wholesale like peace pipes, tomahawks, rattles, Indian headdresses, bow and arrows, dream catchers, mandalas, drums, painted shields and other Native American artifacts.
www.pueblodirect.com

Rubenstein & Ziff

Find American quilting and sewing supplies in Minneapolis, Minnesota, USA. Dealing with trade customers only, supplying a range of wholesale quilting notions, fabric, velcro, fat quarters, quilt patterns, how to books, and related sewing and quiltmaking supplies for art and craft stores.
www.quiltworksonline.com

Arts & Crafts Continued

Sundance Glass

Suppliers of glass art supplies, tools and equipment for artists and artisans working with glass, headquarters in Paradise, California USA. Products include flame working supplies, lampworking products, kilns, glass art starter kits, instruction manuals, glassblowing products, glass, borosilicate products, glass bead making tools, stained glass making tools, torches, glass tubes and rods, casting tools, and other related glass products.
www.sundanceglass.com

Sunshine Joy

Wholesale craft supply distributors in Woonsocket, Rhode Island, in the United States. Distributes a range of fabric paints, clothes spray paint, tie dye supplies, tie dye shirts, tapestries, hippie clothes, wall hangings, and related gifts and general merchandise online.
www.sunshinejoy.com

2Sculpt

American suppliers of sculpting stone and tools for sculptors in Lawrence, Kansas in the United States of America. Provides a range of hand tools for sculpture, carving tools, air tools, diamond blades, abrasives, polishers, sealers, and other sculpture equipment. Also supplies a range of stone for sculpting, like limestone, alabaster, marble, travertine, onyx and other stone materials to sculpt with.
http://2sculpt.com

Jewelry

AAB Style, Inc.

Selection of wholesale body jewelry and body piercing jewelry at below wholesale prices. Online catalog updated regularly by the Plantation, Florida based body jewelry wholesale distributor. Products include navel / belly button jewelry, tongue jewelry, eyebrow rings and barbells, labrets, balls, spikes, ear jewelry, plugs, tusks/talons, eyebrow jewelry, fake body piercings, and belly button rings.
www.aabstyle.com

1Accesorios

Wholesale jewelry company with sterling silver jewelry, 10K gold jewelry, fashion jewelry, body jewelry, and fashion accessories like bracelets and healing crystals.
www.1accesorios.com

All Tribes

Wholesale native American jewelry and accessories in Gilbert, Arizona. Offering closeout jewelry, charms, bracelets, dream catchers, and more.
www.alltribes.com

Jewelry Continued

Ancient Circles

Celtic jewelry supplier based in Willits, California. Offering wholesale celtic products and jewelry that includes ancient spirals, torcs, elemental earrings, medieval belts and girdles, circlets, medallions, the Green man, Nathor, and the Star Goddess jewelry.

www.ancientcircles.com

Awnol.com

Wholesale costume jewelry company located in Harahan, Louisiana. Selling bridal jewelry, Mardi Gras beads, tiaras, rhinestones, charm bracelets, religious jewelry, and more.

www.awnol.com

Fancy Beads

Fancy Beads specializes in importing and selling wholesale beads, clasps and toggles, findings tools, and related items from all over the world. Carrying a full range of wholesale beads including noodle beads, Venetian glass beads, crystal beads, marcasite beads, and seed beads. Jewelry company based in Columbus, Ohio, USA.

www.fancybeads.com

Jewelry Continued

Brand Name Only

Wholesale watches located in Monsey, New York, United States of America. Genuine authentic wholesale watches from premium brands like Tag Heuer, Omega, Breitling, Cartier, Jaeger-LeCoultre and more.
www.brandnameonly.com

Costume Jewelry Wholesale

Retail and wholesale costume jewelry located in Houston, Texas, USA. Includes cowgirl jewelry, cheerleaders, patriotic jewelry and more at wholesale prices.
www.costumejewelrywholesale.com

Cubic Zirconia Wholesale

Wholesale jewelry company in Los Angeles, California, USA with synthetic gemstone and cubic zirconia products. Includes 925 sterling silver jewelry with CZ diamonds and gems on rings, earrings, pendants, bracelets, necklaces and silver chains.
www.cubiczirconiawholesale.com

Jewelry Continued

Diamond on Net
Family owned and operated wholesale diamond business in Los Angeles, California importing, cutting and distributing high quality certified diamonds to jewelry stores. Includes bridal jewelry, diamond rings, necklaces, and more.
www.diamondonnet.com

1 Diamond Source
Wholesale diamonds and diamond jewelry that has been GIA certified. Offering loose diamonds, diamond rings, necklaces, earrings and jewelry from New York City.
www.1diamondsource.com

Double Dee Deals
US jewelry suppliers based in Richmond, Texas in the United States of America. Suppliers of Native American jewelry, turquoise jewelry, bracelets, earrings, necklaces, feather jewelry, dream catchers, pendants, American Indian jewelry sets, men's and women's watches, hair jewelry, zuni fetishes, and silver ethnic North American jewelry.
www.doubledeedeals.com

Jewelry Continued

Egypt 7000

Wholesale Arabian jewelry maker with offices in Egypt and Texas, USA. Supplies handcrafted gold and silver cartouche jewelry, Arab jewelry, Egyptian jewelry, and Arabic lettered jewelry items wholesale.
www.egypt7000.com

Fishing Cross

Company in the USA supplying wholesale Christian jewelry made in the USA. Includes Christian cross necklaces, pendants, key chains and jewelry for Christians and worshipping Jesus Christ. Includes Christian cross jewelry made from bronze, silver, gold, pewter and platinum.
www.fishingcross.com

Girard's Watches

Antique, vintage and new watches and jewelry at wholesale cost from a Pinckney, MI based wholesaler. Specializing in fine platinum, diamonds, antiques, collectibles, Victorian to estate jewelry, watches and gemstones. Also pre-owned wrist and pocket watches from major brands like Rolex, Tudor, Gruen, Longines, Omega, Girard Perregaux, Benrus, Jules Jurgensen, Universal Geneve, Seiko, Cartier, and Tiffany brands.
www.girards.com

Jewelry Continued

Glamour Goddess Jewelry

United States wholesale jeweler in Boca Raton, FL of rhinestone jewelry, bridal jewelry, dance jewelry, and rhinestone tiaras..
www.glamourgoddessjewelry.com

14k Gold Earrings

Wholesale gold jewelry distributer and wholesaler located in Los Angeles, California, United States.
www.14kgoldearrings.com

Jewelry Supply

Wholesale jewelry making supplies with a range of Swarovski crystals, beads, beading supplies, stringing materials, chains and wires, pendants, charms, jewelry tools, jewelry displays, boxes and packaging, and magnifiers for jewelry makers.
www.jewelrysupply.com

Jewelry Continued

Kingdom Wear

American wholesale Christian jewelry company supplying cross necklaces, engraved dog tags, Christian rings for men and women, bracelets, key chains, and related Christianity jewelry products praising god and Christianity.
www.kingdomwear.com

Rings & Things

Wholesale supplier of jewelry findings and beads for professional craftspeople and jewelry makers. Large selection of jewelry-making products from an online store with beads, jewelry findings, charms, cord, polymer clay, Swarovski crystal beads and prisms, Czech glass beads, and jewelry display items, located in Spokane, WA, USA.
www.rings-things.com

Scripture Wear

Religious jewelry wholesalers with a range of Christian pin, lapels, and related jewelry. Scripture Wear is a wholesale company based in Raleigh, North Carolina, America.
www.scripturewear.com

Jewelry Continued

Semi Precious

Large range of retail and wholesale beaded jewelry sent worldwide from Austin, Texas in America. Offering beads in necklaces, earrings, pendants, bracelets, rings and loose beads.

www.semiprecious.com

Shavonne

Tennessee wholesaler of CZ jewelry offering rings, bracelets, watches and more. Includes sterling silver and cubic zirconia jewelry.

www.shavonne.com

Jewelry Continued

Silver Source
Wholesale jewelry supplies and cheap bulk 925 sterling silver jewelry located in Santa Monica, CA, USA.
www.silversource.com

Silver Tribe
American jewelry business based in Scottsdale, Arizona in the United States. Silver Tribe supplies a range of Native Indian jewelry, turquoise jewelry, gems, bracelets, necklaces, earrings, gemstone pendants, southwest jewelry, liquid silver, Hopi kachinas, watches, Native American belt buckles, tear drop necklaces, money clips, keychains and related American Indian jewelry and ethnic gift products.
http://www.silvertribe.com

Spectrums Jewelry
American wholesaler of platinum jewelry located in Hertford, North Carolina USA. Selling a range of platinum engagement rings, bracelets, earrings, rings, and necklaces, also have 18kt gold, 14kt gold and sterling silver.
http://www.spectrumsjewelry.com

Jewelry Continued

Teeda

Wholesale sterling silver jewelry distributer and wholesaler located in Granada Hills, California, United States. Merchandise available includes silver wholesale cz jewelry, wholesale silver rings, earrings, bracelets, necklaces, chains, pendants, charms and more.
http://www.teeda.com

Thunderbird Jewelry

American wholesale company of Native American jewelry located in Gallup, New Mexico, USA. Suppliers of American Indian jewelry, hand crafted jewelry, turquoise jewelry and Indian artifacts wholesale.
http://www.thunderbird-jewelry.com

Tickers Watches

Cheap wholesaler of watches located in Blaine, Washington, USA. Wholesale distributor of affordable fashion watches, mini clocks, and novelty timepieces.
http://www.tickerswatches.com

Jewelry Continued

ToeRings.com

Large selection of island-inspired, custom-fit, 14K gold and sterling silver toe rings for men and women. Toe ring jewelry wholesaler located in Monument, CO, USA.
http://www.toerings.com

Topazery

Antique jewelry collection includes antique jewelry, vintage jewelry, and estate jewelry of timeless, exceptional beauty. Topazery's jewelry collection has antique rings, engagement rings, antique wedding rings, and other antique jewelry from the 1800's to the present. Online store with offices in Atlanta, Georgia, USA.
http://www.topazery.com

Touch of Avalon

Wholesale and drop ship manufacturer, located in Washington USA offers unique handcrafted jewelry crafted with semiprecious gemstones, sterling silver and crystal.
http://www.touchofavalon.com

Jewelry Continued

Wholesale Wholesale

Wholesale jewelry, rhinestones, fashion jewelry, beads, and costume jewelry from a wholesaler based in Los Angeles, California, USA.
http://www.wholesalewholesale.com

World of Fine Watches

Authentic brand name watches wholesaler based in Encino, California, USA. Selling premium watches from Anonimo, Baume & Mercier, Bell & Ross, Chanel, Gucci watches, Ice Tek, Longines, Michele, Omega, TAG Heuer watch and more.
http://www.worldoffinewatches.com

Other Sources

EBay is another great source for wholesale lots. Read the listing carefully and don't throw a bid out without doing your research first. You can ask the seller questions before bidding too. www.ebay.com

Seleon

Wholesale gold jewelry company in Ontario, Canada. Offering a large selection of wholesale and closeout gold jewelry to retailers and the trade. Also operating a gold jewelry drop shipping program for eBay sellers and website owners. http://www.seleon.ca

Closing

Starting a new business and adding new products is an exciting time but also can be nerve wracking.

I hope this directory saves you considerable time in researching the various whole sale companies available.

I wish you the best of luck with your new venture!

Here's to your success!

Notes

www.ingramcontent.com/pod-product-compliance
Lightning Source LLC
Chambersburg PA
CBHW081504200326
41518CB00015B/2379